NEW ENGLAND

Cathy McManus

Twenty Cases That
Rocked the Region

SCHIFFER
PUBLISHING

Published by Schiffer Publishing, Ltd.
4880 Lower Valley Road
Atglen, PA 19310
Phone: (610) 593-1777; Fax: (610) 593-2002
E-mail: Info@schifferbooks.com
Web: www.schifferbooks.com

For our complete selection of fine books on this and related subjects, please visit our website at www.schifferbooks.com. You may also write for a free catalog.

Schiffer Publishing's titles are available at special discounts for bulk purchases for sales promotions or premiums. Special editions, including personalized covers, corporate imprints, and excerpts, can be created in large quantities for special needs. For more information, contact the publisher.

We are always looking for people to write books on new and related subjects. If you have an idea for a book, please contact us at:

proposals@schifferbooks.com.

To all the families and friends
who have lost someone.
I hope you find your answers and peace.

ACKNOWLEDGMENTS

This book would not have been possible without the support of my family and friends; their understanding and encouragement have made all this possible. To the great people at the historical societies, libraries, and town offices I have contacted—your dedication is keeping our history alive and I think you are wonderful! Also, to my wonderful editor, Dinah Roseberry—she deserves an award for answering all my silly questions—and the rest of the gang at Schiffer Publishing!

Thanks to my family for all their support. To my parents, Jim and Claudette McManus, whose support was instrumental in keeping me sane as I moved and wrote a book at the same time. Thanks to David and Lora McManus, Dan and Kim McManus, and Matt and James McManus. You guys are awesome. Thanks to my extended family—all my cousins, uncles, and aunts. Together we make the best group of weirdos in the world. To my coworkers, especially Tom Callahan, Scott Hall, and Jaime Ela—you guys are basically tolerable. ;-)

Finally, I want to thank all of my friends and followers online, primarily on Facebook—the ideas and support you all provided helped me in more ways than I can say.

CONTENTS

CONNECTICUT
Matthew Margolies Murder (Greenwich) 7
Connecticut Circus Fire (Hartford) 12
The Murder of Father Hubert Dahme (Bridgeport) 19

MAINE
The Murder of Mattie Hackett (Readfield) 24
Sarah Ware's Murder (Bucksport) 27
The Kurt Newton Disappearance (Chain of Ponds) 31

MASSACHUSETTS
The Borden Murders (Fall River) 37
The Great Plymouth Mail Truck Robbery 47
Isabella Stewart Gardner Museum (Boston) 51

NEW HAMPSHIRE
Bear Brook Murders (Allenstown) 62
The Connecticut River Valley Killer (Vermont and New Hampshire) 69

RHODE ISLAND
Camilla "Cam" Lyman's Murder (Hopkinton) 83
Sunny von Bülow's Attempted Murder
or Unfortunate Accident (Newport) 86
The Murder of Rita Bouchard (Pawtucket/Providence) 91

VERMONT
Paula Welden
(One of the People to Go Missing in the Bennington Triangle) 98
The Disappearance of Lynne Schulze (Middlebury) 103

PARANORMAL AND UNEXPLAINED PHENOMENA
Ramtail Factory Site—Ghosts 108
The Betty and Barney Hill Abduction—Aliens 114
Little Rose Ferron—Religion 123
America's Stonehenge—Archeology 127

Conclusion 135
Bibliography 136
Index 140

CONNECTICUT

MATTHEW MARGOLIES MURDER

Greenwich

....

THERE'S NO TRAGEDY IN LIFE LIKE THE DEATH OF A CHILD.
THINGS NEVER GET BACK TO THE WAY THEY WERE.

—DWIGHT D. EISENHOWER

Greenwich, Connecticut, must have seemed like a small piece of heaven to the Margolies family. A place where nothing bad could ever happen, where young Matthew Margolies could indulge in his favorite activity, fishing. Where, in the end, it all went horribly wrong.

The Byram River not far from where Matthew's body was found in Greenwich, Connecticut

7

August 31, 1984, was another brilliant summer day in the Valley. Many people saw Matthew that day working his way to different fishing spots along the Byram River. After he'd spent the morning fishing, he'd dropped off a trout at his grandmother's home. Then he changed out of his wet clothes, leaving a mess behind for his grandmother, Stella Miazga, to deal with when she got home. At 5:00 p.m., locals saw him within a block of the Sparta Deli, a popular hangout for the local kids. At 5:30 p.m., a young woman saw Matthew walking on Comly Street, and they waved to each other.

Matthew was never seen alive again. There were reports that he may have gotten into a car belonging to one of the Valley Boys, a group of older kids known in the area as troublemakers, but the police could not verify this.

As the sun set that night, Maryann Margolies, Matthew's mother, began calling around the neighborhood. Matthew hadn't come home for dinner. The news spread quickly in the small community. Then a couple of Matthew's friends reported that he'd failed to meet up with them as planned to go fishing that afternoon. The townsfolk organized a search that evening. Most people felt something was not right, but they were hopeful that Matthew might have gone off to think. In the past year, Matthew had lost much. His parents had gotten divorced, and his father had moved away to Texas. Then his fishing buddy and grandfather, George Miazga, had recently died of cancer. Many thought, or hoped, that Matthew had gone off to be alone for a while. However, no one believed that he would take off. Not without leaving a message for his mother and grandmother.

The days that followed the disappearance saw a huge manhunt in the Valley, the local name for the Pembrook area of Greenwich. Helicopters combed the area from above, people searched on the ground, and Maryann even took Matthew's dog along the river paths, hoping he would lead her to Matthew. The police also had scuba divers explore the pond above the nearby falls. On September 3, Matthew's older sister, Stacey, even contacted a psychic to aid in the search. The psychic predicted that an unknown male would find Matthew's body nearby on a steep hill. She was proven right two days after this terrible prediction.

A volunteer firefighter, Frank Lambert, was searching a steep wooded ridge overlooking Pembrook Drive. He first found the sneakers that Matthew had been wearing on the day he'd disappeared. He left immediately to fetch police officers Steven Paulo and Michael Panzer. Frank then led the officers back to the area where he had found the sneakers. They followed the scent of decay and swarms of flies and soon found Matthew's body partially covered on the slope. His body had been covered with dirt and debris.

Matthew was clothed only in his underwear and one sock. He had been stabbed in the chest and abdomen, and his white T-shirt was knotted around his neck. The killer had also shoved dirt, twigs, and Matthew's other sock down his throat. His neck had been cut as well.

Upon the discovery of Matthew's body, there was a drastic change in the Valley. The area that had been bustling with activity and sociable neighbors was now a ghost town. Whoever did this was out there and most likely local. Before Matthew's

A fishing spot along the Byram River in Greenwich, Connecticut

death, kids played in the park or at the area's athletic fields; afterward, people started locking their cars and homes at night. There was a child killer out there and he could be your neighbor. How could you feel safe?

Almost immediately the police came under fire. Many felt that waiting until after Matthew's body had been found to begin investigating the crime was a mistake. Too much time had passed. Matthew's killer had time to cover his tracks and distance himself from the crime. It didn't help that there had been another unsolved, at the time, murder in Greenwich. Almost nine years before, someone murdered fifteen-year-old Martha Moxley, and her killer was still on the loose. Now, another of the town's children was dead, and the police weren't making any headway on either case. Residents believed that many leads were not properly followed up on, and too many people were not thoroughly investigated.

For example, a "friend" of Matthew's was found with Matthew's fishing rod. Police stated that the young man claimed that Matthew had sold him the rod. The police stated, "The holder of the rod was not a material witness or suspect," despite Maryann's insistence that Matthew would never part with the rod—it had been a There was also a local boy, Jeff Payne, who had been assaulted in a similar fashion as Matthew. An older boy bullied and cajoled Jeff to go with him for a soda. At first, Jeff refused, not liking the way the older boy was looking at him, but he soon relented. Jeff was driven to a house, and the boys went into the basement. After checking if the coast was clear, the older boy attacked Jeff, slamming his head into the tile floor. He then proceeded to torture him, driving nails into his back and cutting him with broken glass. Then just when he told Jeff to pull down his pants, the house's tenants came back, thus saving Jeff from possible rape and murder. The boy cleaned up Jeff and returned him home. Once Jeff was alone with his mother, he broke down and told her of his ordeal. The police arrested the older boy and took him to court. However, this older boy was not behind bars at the time of Matthew's death. Jeff is convinced that his torturer killed Matthew. The police did look at this boy, but he had an alibi for the time of Matthew's death. So he was released. The police were getting nowhere, and their only description of Matthew's killer: "white male."

The case was at a standstill until, in 2000, the Connecticut Cold Case Squad decided to investigate the murder. They felt confident that they would be able to catch Matthew's murderer. The evidence had been well preserved and they had a list of "persons of interest." They narrowed in on Roger Bates, a police officer of Port Chester, which was the next town over, located in New York. Bates was convicted in Texas of child molestation, and he had ties to Matthew. During Bates's 2004 molestation trial, the son of another Port Chester police officer came forward and testified that Roger Bates had molested him. He also testified that on at least one occasion, the officer had taken him and Matthew fishing on the river. Bates was interviewed by police and his DNA was tested, but it did not match the DNA found at the crime scene. In 2006, a grand jury denied the request to indict Roger Bates for Matthew's murder.

At the time of writing this book, it has been over thirty-two years since that bright day in Greenwich. Maryann Margolies still lives in the same house, and she still holds out hope that Matthew's murderer will be found.

A reward has been offered for any information leading to the arrest and conviction of the person who murdered Matthew Margolies. If you have any information about this case, please contact the Greenwich Police Department at (203) 622-8000.

|||||||||||||||||||||||||||||||||||||||||||||||||||||||||||||||||||||||||||||||||||||||||||||

Martha Moxley

On October 30, 1975, Martha Moxley was out celebrating "Mischief Night"—a night dedicated to pranks and misbehavior that has escalated in some areas to vandalism and arson—at a neighbor's home. The fifteen-year-old lived in the well-to-do neighborhood of Belle Haven in Greenwich. That evening, partygoers saw Martha flirting with and kissing Thomas Skakel, one of the boys who lived in the home where the party was being held.

On Friday morning, a schoolmate found Martha's body under a tree in her family's backyard. Someone had beaten her with a golf club until the shaft broke into pieces, then stabbed her with the broken shaft. Her pants and underwear had been pulled down, but she had not been sexually assaulted.

The police focused on Thomas and Michael Skakel, the boys who had thrown the "Mischief Night" party. The golf club that had been used to kill Martha was from the Skakel home, and both boys had an interest in Martha. However, their father did not allow them to be interrogated by police, so they weren't able to fully follow up on their suspicions.

Over the years, the boys' alibis changed, with Michael even claiming at one point to have masturbated in a tree in the Moxleys' yard that evening.

It wasn't until 1998 that a grand jury indicted Michael Skakel. The prosecution had several witness who claimed that Michael had bragged about getting away with the murder. As a relative of the politically powerful Kennedy family (a Kennedy cousin), he allegedly claimed that he was untouchable. The courts decided to try Michael Skakel as an adult (despite his being fifteen at the time of the murder), and the court convicted him on June 7, 2002. The court sentenced him to twenty years to life in prison.

The story doesn't end here though. Michael began the appeals process in the courts while the Kennedy family fought for him in the court of public opinion. Skakel's appeals were repeatedly turned down, and Connecticut's Supreme Court refused his petition for a retrial. His first bid for parole was also denied in 2012.

In October 2013, a Connecticut judge ruled that Michael had not been adequately represented in his trial, and Skakel was released on bail the following month. In December 2016, the Connecticut Supreme Court reinstated his conviction. On May 4, 2018, before he could be returned to prison, the Connecticut Supreme Court reversed its decision and vacated his conviction. Prosecutors have decided not to retry the case.

The Kennedys maintain his innocence, while the Moxley family believes that Michael is the person who brutally murdered their daughter/sister.

|||||||||||||||||||||||||||||||||||||||||||||||||||||||||||||||||||||||||||||||

CONNECTICUT CIRCUS FIRE

Hartford

....

LADIES AND GENTLEMEN, BOYS AND GIRLS, CHILDREN OF
ALL AGES, GET READY FOR THE GREATEST SHOW ON EARTH!

—RINGMASTER

One of the great experiences of childhood is going to the circus. Even for someone with coulrophobia (the fear of clowns), there is so much to see—so many bright colors and flashing lights. There are acts of amazing skill and bravery, high-wire acts, large exotic animals, and, yes, clowns. The sights, sounds, and smells all add to the building excitement. Add some spun sugar and popcorn, and a variety of other fun treats, and this all adds up to a perfect diversion.

This event takes place on July 6, 1944, and a distraction was something that everyone could use. The US was fighting World War II, and so many indulgences were being rationed. What better way for the people of Hartford to take their minds off war than to watch the Great Wallendas, a famous high-wire act now known as the Flying Wallendas, or watch Emmett Kelly, the ultimate sad hobo clown, and a wide variety of exotic acts for an hour or more? The war made things tough for the circus as well, though. There was a shortage of men to work, they couldn't get all the supplies they once could, and travel by rail could be interrupted in order for the government to move troops or supplies across the country. In fact, the train had been running late and the first show on July 5 had to be canceled. The folks at Ringling Brothers and Barnum & Bailey circus were able to get everything set up so that the evening performance on the fifth went on as scheduled. There is an old circus superstition that canceling a show is a bad omen, but there was nothing that they could do.

The afternoon show on the sixth was going well. The lions had finished their act, and the Great Wallendas were performing. It was twenty minutes into the show when bandleader Merle Evans spotted the flames along the southwestern sidewall of the tent. He began to play "The Stars and Stripes Forever," the traditional

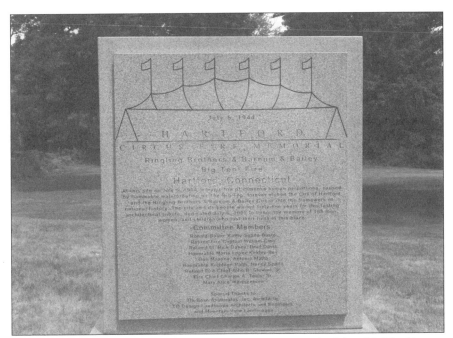

Memorial at the entrance to the Hartford Circus Fire Memorial site. Behind the Wish School in Hartford.

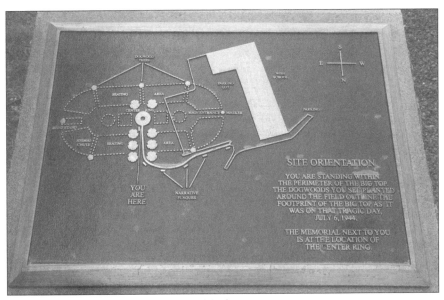

A map of the layout of the circus on the day of the fire

The pathway leading to the center of the memorial. It is lined with narrative plaques with a timeline of the day's events.

Memorial marker for the graves of the unknown victims of the circus fire, at Northwood Cemetery in Windsor, Connecticut

distress signal for circus employees. Ringmaster Frank Branda tried to calm the crowd and direct an orderly evacuation, but the power in the tent failed and no one could hear him over the crowd. There were 7,500 to 8,700 people attending the matinee that day, and it was pandemonium as everyone tried to escape the flames. Two of the exits were blocked at the time of the fire because the big-cat chutes were still in place. So people were desperate to find other ways out. Some managed to crawl under the canvas sidewalls, others cut their way through the canvas, but many were trapped. To make things worse, the tent's top canvas had been soaked in a mixture of Texaco white gas and yellow paraffin wax to make the top waterproof (they had not treated the sidewalls with the mixture). This created the problem of burning hot wax raining down on the already terrified crowd. After only eight minutes the tent collapsed, trapping hundreds of people underneath.

Actor, comedian, and director Charles Nelson Reilly was there that day. In *The Life of Reilly*, a film adaptation of his one-man play *Save It for the Stage: The Life of Riley*, he tells us about that day. His thirteen-year-old friend Donald Baggish had received free tickets to the show and invited Charles to come along. Charles's mother forbade her son to go, since his father had also bought tickets, and he was going to be taking Charles to the evening performance. Being a typical kid, Charles decided he didn't want to wait to go with his father and snuck off with Donald.

The marker at the location where the center ring of the tent was located

The field where the circus set up on the day of the fire

His mother saw them leaving the neighborhood and yelled at the boys, "I hope it burns to the ground!"

Charles tells of the excitement of seeing the wild animals, the hush of the crowd as they anticipated the beginning of the Great Wallendas performance, and the terror they felt when they spotted the fire. Both Charles and Donald ran from the tent and didn't stop until they'd reached the far end of the parking lot. When they turned around, the tent had burned to rubble, and he recalls a young girl running by with her face nearly burnt off. He ends this story with "Donald never said what my mother had yelled from the porch that morning . . . Donald was a good friend." He later said he avoided attending the theater because the sounds of the audience reminded him of the circus.

The official death toll was 168 people, with over 700 people being seriously hurt and seeking medical treatment that day. The true numbers are believed to be higher. In the official tally, one victim was a collection of body parts that didn't go with any of the other victims. Also, many of the injured did not seek immediate medical attention because they were in shock and had wandered off the site to go home. Additionally, there was the problem that the circus had given away many tickets. Transients were often given tickets to fill up the Big Top. So the number of attendees could have been higher than records show.

The next step was to identify the dead. There were morgues set up around town, and in the end, of the bodies found, six remained unidentified—three adults and three children. They were assigned numbers, and on July 10, they were buried at public expense. A Jewish rabbi, a Catholic priest, and a Protestant minister all said prayers for the dead. There are still efforts to identify them.

||||||||||||||||||||||||||||||||||||||||||||||||||||||||||||||||||||||||||||||||

Little Miss 1565

Little Miss 1565 was the most famous victim of the Hartford, Connecticut, circus fire: a young blonde girl with almost no marks on her face. She was about seven years old. She was not identified, and the town buried her with the other unknown victims at Northwood Cemetery in Windsor, Connecticut. Her story has been told again and again. Hartford police sergeants Thomas Barber and Edward Lowe were determined to find out who she was. They had dental impressions made and sent them out to dentists; they interviewed everyone they could and even sent letters with a picture of the girl to elementary schools. The two men visited her grave every Christmas and Memorial Day. They were never able to identify the child though. In 1987, someone left a note on the gravestone, claiming "Sarah Graham is her name! 7-6-38 DOB, 6 years, Twin." Other notes

Little Miss 1565 marker at Northwood Cemetery in Windsor, Connecticut

claimed that her twin and family were buried nearby, but nothing has come of this information.

Then, in 1991, an author claimed the girl was Eleanor Cook and went so far as to have her body exhumed, then reburied, in Southampton, Massachusetts—all this despite Little Miss 1565's dental records not matching. Eleanor's mother always believed that Little Miss 1565 was not her daughter.

Stewart O'Nan, author of *The Circus Fire: A True Story of American Tragedy*, believes that Little Miss 1565's family may have claimed Eleanor's body by mistake, thinking she was their little one, thus leaving her unclaimed and Eleanor's family without her remains.

‖‖

The official cause of the fire was listed as "undetermined." Some believe that it was a cigarette that smoldered and eventually lit the canvas on fire. Others believe it was arson. However it started, there needed to be an investigation, and there needed to be someone to blame. On July 7, charges of involuntary manslaughter were brought against five officials and employees of Ringling Brothers. The circus agreed to accept full financial responsibility and to pay whatever the city requested in damages, which turned out to be $5,000,000 to the 600 victims and families who filed claims. All of the circus's profits from 1944 to 1954 went to pay this debt.

While the circus accepted financial responsibility, it did not accept blame for the disaster itself. However, the courts found four out of the five men charged with involuntary manslaughter guilty. They were sentenced to prison. Despite the conviction, they were allowed to continue with the circus to Sarasota, Florida, to help set up after the disaster. The four men received pardons not long after their conviction.

Memorial bricks dedicated to survivors and victims of the fire

The question is how did the fire start? Ringling Brothers stated that the canvas sidewall was often charred by cigarettes or cigars. It is inevitable that would happen with such large crowds, but it had never resulted in flames. Only if a flame is directly applied to the canvas would a fire start.

Then, on June 26, 1950, Robert Segee confessed to deliberately setting the Hartford fire. He also confessed to setting two previous fires as the circus traveled. He was in Ohio facing two counts of arson there when he confessed. Segee was fourteen years old and worked as a roustabout for the circus. He said he would have nightmares about an Indian riding a flaming horse who told him to start fires. Once he had the dream he would be in an almost trancelike state until he did what the nightmare had commanded. He knew a lot of details about the fires, but as a circus employee, it isn't unusual that he would know these things. He told officials that he confessed to the circus fire because he dreamt of a woman standing in flames and urging him to confess. He was convicted of the two counts of arson in Ohio and was sentenced to forty years in prison. Connecticut officials were never allowed to interview Segee, and his confession, which he recanted soon after, was not considered legitimate.

As for the circus, they returned to touring on August 4, 1944, performing at the Rubber Bowl in Akron, Ohio. This was the first time their show had not been staged under their main tent. As for returning to Connecticut, the next time Ringling Brothers and Barnum & Bailey performed in the state was in 1975, over forty years later. They did not use a tent though.

THE MURDER OF FATHER HUBERT DAHME

Bridgeport

....

[I]T IS JUST AS IMPORTANT FOR A STATE'S ATTORNEY TO USE
THE GREAT POWERS OF HIS OFFICE TO PROTECT THE
INNOCENT AS IT IS TO CONVICT THE GUILTY.

—HOMER CUMMINGS

At 7:30 on the evening of February 4, 1924, Father Hubert Dahme left his rectory. He was the priest of St. Joseph's Roman Catholic Church in Bridgeport. Almost every evening saw the father going for a walk, and tonight was no exception. He told his housekeeper, as he was heading out the door, that he'd be back in five minutes. It isn't known what path the priest took, but this evening someone was following him as he walked toward Main Street. Several witnesses saw the stranger quicken his pace as they approached the intersection at High Street. When the man caught up to Father Dahme, he raised a .32-caliber revolver to the back of the priest's head and shot him. Onlookers say the man said something "derogatory" to Father Dahme right before he fired, but no one heard exactly what was said. As the father crumpled to the sidewalk, the shooter ran up High Street.

This killer was incredibly bold. Not only had he shot Father Dahme on a well-lit public street, but there were a large number of police and theatergoers around, since the spot was near the Palace and the Majestic Theaters. In the chaos that followed, it was almost ten minutes before medical attention was sought for Father Dahme. Medics took him to St. Vincent's Hospital, where he died two hours later.

At first the police were sure it was a "drug-addled maniac" who killed the priest, and they rounded up all the addicts they could find in the area. One of the men interviewed had recently been fired from a construction job at St. Joseph's, but the police concluded that the man did not have a grudge against Father Dahme. The police soon released him.

Downtown Bridgeport, Connecticut

There were the eyewitnesses, though. They described the killer as a thirty-five-year-old man, wearing a blue or dark-gray cap pulled down low over his eyes and a gray overcoat. Not much to go on.

There was also the issue of motive. No one could think of a reason why Father Dahme was targeted. He was popular with his parish and was, by all accounts, a mild-mannered man. Theories ran wild. Had someone gone to confession, and was he concerned that the priest would break the seal of silence? A priest vows to never reveal what he hears during confession. However, the killer may have still feared that the priest would tell the police of a horrible deed. There were no clues . . . other than the people who actually saw the murder.

On February 12, the police arrested their suspect, twenty-year-old Harold Israel. Israel was an Army veteran who had been arrested in Norwalk, Connecticut, for illegally having a concealed weapon—a .32-caliber revolver. When four of the seven witnesses identified Israel as Father Dahme's murderer, he was taken in for questioning, and after over twenty-eight hours of intense interrogation, Harold Israel confessed to murdering Father Dahme.

This is where prosecutor Homer Cummings, the state's attorney for Fairfield County, enters the picture. When he was first given the case, Cummings thought it was an easy conviction despite Israel recanting his confession. Homer Cummings, though, was a man of integrity, and the more he looked at the case, the more problems he found with it. Ballistic reports that indicated that Israel's gun was the murder weapon were disproved by ballistic experts. When Cummings spoke with medical experts, they all agreed. After such an extended interview, Israel would have confessed to whatever he was accused of just to be allowed to sleep.

Main Street, Bridgeport, Connecticut, where Father Dahme was shot

Grave of Homer Cummings in Woodland Cemetery

As for the eyewitnesses, Cummings interviewed each person and found them to be either unsure of their identification or unreliable. He even went so far as to go to the scene of the crime and stand where the witnesses had stood. In the case of a waitress who had seen the gunman run past her workplace, there were two panels of glass between where she stood and the street. The glare from the diner's lights prevented the identification of anyone on the street. When Cummings spoke with her, she could not be certain it was Israel she had seen. One witness described the gun used to shoot Father Dahme as black, but Israel's gun was chrome and would have glittered in the street lights. While at the scene, Cummings noted that two of the witnesses were too far away to recognize someone they knew, never mind be able to identify a stranger. The final witness had changed their testimony and was not considered reliable.

On May 27, 1924, Homer Cummings went to Bridgeport's courtroom and shocked everyone when he dropped the charges against Harold Israel. He presented his findings to the court, and the former soldier was released from custody.

Homer Cummings was hailed as a hero who had saved a soldier from prison. Cummings was later heavily involved in politics and was Franklin D. Roosevelt's attorney general from 1933 to 1939. He was also the hero of Elia Kazan's 1947 movie *Boomerang!*, about his efforts to free Harold Israel. He even negotiated with Twentieth Century Fox on behalf of Israel for the rights to his story, thus ensuring Israel would have financial security for his family. Cummings donated his royalties from the movie to the George Washington University Hospital.

After police released Harold Israel, they did continue to investigate the case, but no arrests have ever been made. The town of Bridgeport has not forgotten this seemingly senseless act and has screenings of *Boomerang!* at the local library and movie theaters. Still, now over ninety years after the murder, no one has any idea who walked up to Father Dahme on a busy street and murdered him.

Maine

THE MURDER OF MATTIE HACKETT

Readfield

ON AUGUST 17, 1905, YOUR FAMILY'S LEFT TO CROON.
MATTIE, ONLY SEVENTEEN. THE SEARCH WENT ON SO LONG.
OLDEST UNSOLVED MYSTERY.
SO I WROTE IT DOWN IN SONG.

—ELLEN BOWMAN, "ODE TO MATTIE HACKETT"

The Hackett family grave at the Readfield Corner Cemetery

Mattie Hackett was a bright and promising seventeen-year-old girl who lived on a farm with her parents in Kent's Hill, just outside Readfield, Maine. On August 17, 1905, things all went tragically wrong for the family. Early in the evening, Mrs. Hackett went to a neighbor's house for a visit, and Mr. Hackett was in the stable with Albert Johnson, a tramp who was looking for a place to stay or work. Mattie was in the house, cleaning the dinner dishes. When Mr. Hackett returned to the home, Mattie was no longer in the house. He heard a disturbance down the road and hurried along the road that ran along the farm to check it out. About 275 yards from the house, he found Mattie on the ground; she was barely conscious.

Someone went to get Mattie's mother from the neighbor's house, and they brought Mattie inside the

Marker for the grave of Mattie Hackett

farmhouse. Unfortunately, it was too dark on the road for her father to see the cord that was still tightly tied around her throat, and Mattie died while they carried her back into the home.

The police arrested Mr. Johnson for "having knowledge" of the murder. However, it was quickly discovered that he could only have been a witness to events. Authorities held him in Augusta's county jail for almost two months. They knew he was a transient, and didn't want to give him the opportunity to disappear. He was released when officials decided that any information Mr. Johnson had was not going to be useful.

While the police were unable to gather sufficient evidence to take someone to trial, there was a person most everyone in town suspected. Townsfolk said Mrs. Elise Hobbs Raymond was terribly jealous of Mattie. This rumor started because when both Elise and her future husband worked at the Readfield Hotel, they would have frequent contact with Mattie. Mr. Raymond had even been rumored to have gone driving with Mattie. The theory is that Elise Raymond was jealous of the flirtation her boyfriend may have had with the pretty young woman.

There were also other indications that Elise may have been involved in Mattie's murder. There were witnesses who saw a woman in a brown dress walking along the road that Mattie had been murdered on. Also, at the time of the attack, Elise had not been at home. Her husband and his brothers had been looking for her since she had run off after the couple had had an argument. Additionally, there were tracks found in the gutter at the murder site. They were small and believed to belong to a woman. Another clue was a library book that Elise had taken out from the public library. In it, there was a tale of an Australian murder that was similar to the way Mattie had been killed.

Elise proclaimed her innocence to any who would listen. She did not own a brown dress, and her shoes did not match the prints found at the scene of the crime. She claimed to have spent the evening of the murder in the orchard out behind the tenement where she lived. That is where her husband found her at about eleven that night.

For seven years, Elise lived under the suspicion of the area's residents, and Mattie's family lived without knowing who had killed their daughter. In 1912, Elise was indicted for the murder. The papers made much of the fact that Elise, now a mother, had her four-year-old daughter clinging to her as the police came to take her to jail. Elise's daughter, Evelyn, was taken away by her father so she would not see her mother locked up behind bars. According to the papers, even the jailers were moved to tears.

The trauma of being separated from her family notwithstanding, Elise welcomed the chance to prove her innocence. Both she and her husband believed that authorities would clear this matter up once and for all. At this time they had already seen two grand juries fail to indict her for the crime. However, recently a man had come forward saying he could identify the woman in brown as Elise.

The trial consisted of only circumstantial evidence, and it took the jury only two hours to acquit Elise. There have been no other suspects in the case, and to this day we don't know what happened to poor Mattie Hackett.

SARAH WARE'S MURDER

Bucksport

....

SOCIETY WANTS TO BELIEVE IT CAN IDENTIFY EVIL PEOPLE,
OR HARMFUL PEOPLE, BUT IT'S NOT PRACTICAL. THERE ARE
NO STEREOTYPES.

—THEODORE BUNDY

Bucksport is a small mill town at the head of the Penobscot Bay. It has a curious history, with haunted forts, lost native tribes, witch's curses, and rampaging circus elephants. The town certainly doesn't lack color. However, most of the town's color seems to be of the darker variety. One of the darkest moments involves the gruesome beheading of one of its residents, and the possible conspiracy of the town's people to cover up who killed her.

Late in the evening of September 17, 1898, fifty-two-year-old divorcée Sarah Ware was observed hurrying home. That was the last confirmed sighting of her, alive. At first, people didn't really notice Sarah was gone, and if they did notice, they thought she may have just left town. For whatever reason, she was not reported missing for at least a week (some reports claim it was two weeks). Sarah's body was found on the second of October. She was laid out in a pasture not far from her home. The reports claimed that the searchers smelled her before they saw her. The body was highly decomposed, and when they picked it up to move it to the coroner's office, her head fell off.

At the coroner's inquest it was ruled as death by other than natural causes / death by violence. Her attacker(s) had smashed the left side of her face to a bloody pulp, and they had severed her neck. The three attending doctors could not agree on what weapon had caused the damage. The entire state was in an uproar, horrified that such a thing could happen in small-town Maine.

On November 27, stove maker William Treworgy was implicated in the murder. In his cart, authorities found a bloody tarp and a hammer with the initials *WTT* stenciled on the hammer's handle. In fact, there were reports that the head of the

The road where Sarah's body was found

hammer matched the wound in Sarah's head. Only the next day, the investigation stopped. They had run out of money. Community members pooled together $500 so detectives could continue the investigation.

In the spring of 1899, police arrested Treworgy after a local boy, Joseph Fogg Jr., came forward. He said Treworgy had paid him to help move a body the day Sarah Ware had died.

Three years went by before the case came to its final trial. In July 1902, the Hancock County Supreme Court in Ellsworth heard the case. Only by now, the deputy sheriff and the undertaker who had handled the case were dead, and Joseph Fogg Jr. had recanted his testimony. Even worse, evidence had disappeared! Somehow the hammer was gone from the police's storage. They still had Sarah's head, but not the weapon. With the lack of evidence and witnesses, William Treworgy was acquitted of murder.

There is a lot of suspicion about what happened with the evidence and why the testimony was recanted. There were rumors that said Treworgy had a lot of incriminating evidence against powerful people in the town, so they conspired to hide his crime for him. No one else was ever suspected of the murder of Sarah Ware.

There are many theories about what happened to Sarah that September night.

One theory is that Sarah, who worked odd jobs in the town, was collecting money owed her and that her last stop the night was at William Treworgy's home. Emeric Spooner, author of *In Search of Sarah Ware: Reinvestigating Murder and Conspiracy in a Maine Village* and *Sarah Ware Revisited*, believes that Treworgy became enraged at Sarah's demand for payment and beat her to death. Treworgy

Silver Lake Cemetery; it is rumored that Sarah's body may have been secretly moved here.

had a quick and violent temper. He was well known for his ornery ways. His threat to take down everyone with him if he was convicted does cast even more suspicion on him. Did Treworgy indeed have blackmail materials on people in the town? There has been no proof found (although good blackmail material would be hard to find).

Maybe there was more than one person involved in Sarah's murder. Another theory is that a group of young men accosted Sarah that night on Miles Lane, and they attacked and murdered her.

Still others believe that Sarah went out to the pasture and committed suicide, then a cow stepped on her head, crushing her skull.

Even more far-fetched is this last theory: some people believe that Sarah Ware was the Bucksport Witch. Sarah was either possessed by her or a reincarnation of her, and that, somehow, led to her death.

||||||||||||||||||||||||||||||||||||||||||||||||||||||||||||||||||||||||||||||||||||||||||||

A Witch's Curse

Bucksport has a history of historical oddities, one of which is the curse of a witch whom townsfolk burned at the stake by order of Colonel Jonathan Buck. The witch cursed the town as she burned. She vowed she would come back to dance on Buck's grave, and if one views the tombstone of Colonel Buck, there is an imperfection in the shape of a leg on it. Some believe this is proof of the witch's curse. Although, how this possession would lead to Sarah's death is unclear to me. As for the witch's curse, Sarah seems like an unlikely victim for a witch persecuted by men.

||||||||||||||||||||||||||||||||||||||||||||||||||||||||||||||||||||||||||||||||||||||||

There is one other mystery surrounding Sarah Ware, and that is the location of her body. Her headstone is in Oak Hill Cemetery, but the rumors are that Sarah's daughter, Mildred, had her mother's body moved to Silver Lane Cemetery so that no one would disturb her grave. However, the grave at Oak Hill Cemetery is not empty. The state kept Sarah's head at the Ellsworth courthouse as evidence in case there was another trial. It was discovered in 1982, and then, on the one hundredth anniversary of Sarah's death, her head was buried at the Oak Hill site. This separation of head and body may be why there are rumors that Sarah is haunting the streets of Bucksport. People say you can see her walking to a home she will never reach.

It is no wonder she is restless. Not only has her killer never been brought to justice, but her remains may not even be interred in one place.

The grave of Sarah Ware in Oak Hill Cemetery

THE KURT NEWTON DISAPPEARANCE

Chain of Ponds

....

THERE IS NO FRIENDSHIP, NO LOVE, LIKE THAT OF THE
PARENT FOR THE CHILD.

—HENRY WARD BEECHER

It was late August in the summer of 1975 when four families from Manchester, Maine, decided to spend Labor Day weekend at Natanis Point Campground in Chain of Ponds, Maine, about one hundred miles north of their homes. The campground, located only six miles from the Canadian border, is nestled into the woods not far from where the paper companies were cutting down trees. There were almost sixty sites at this campground, and there is nearly every summer outdoor activity available—a perfect place for everyone to relax and have some fun.

One of the families, the Newtons, was especially enthusiastic about the trip. They had just bought a secondhand tent trailer and were anxious to try it out. For Jill and Ron Newton, everything seemed to be going right. They had been married for eight years and had a home directly across the street from the elementary school their children would someday go. But children: that is where they felt they had been most blessed. They'd wanted two children, a boy and a girl, and that is what they had. Kimberly was six years old that summer and would be starting first grade, and there was four-year-old Kurt.

The Newtons got to the campground on Friday, August 29. The family set up their site and gathered wood for a bonfire. It all started as an idyllic weekend. The kids raced their bikes along the dirt logging roads, and everyone came together for meals and the nightly campfire.

On Sunday, August 30, the morning air was chilly, and the mist hung low near the two ponds that bordered the campground. Ron started another fire to ward off the chill, and after a hearty breakfast the family split up to do their own things. Kimberly was playing a game, Jill went down to the bathhouse to clean off muddy

Natanis Point Campground in Chain of Ponds

sneakers, and Ron jumped into his Bronco, heading to chop some more firewood. Everyone thought that Kurt was just riding his tricycle around near the campsite.

One of the other campers heard Kurt calling after his father as Ron left to get wood. No one knew that the little boy had jumped on his tricycle and started after his father's truck. About a quarter mile away from the campsite, a young girl, Lou Ellen Hanson, saw Kurt pedaling as fast as he could down the road, away from camp. Lou Ellen yelled to him, asking if his parents knew where he was. This is the last anyone has seen of Kurt Newton that we know about.

It took Jill Newton about ten minutes to clean the kids' shoes and hang them on the line to dry. When she got back to the family's campsite, she didn't see Kurt or his tricycle. She and a friend started checking with other campers. When no one there had seen him, she thought he must have gone with his father to chop wood. At this time, she met up with Jack Hanson, who volunteered as a caretaker at the campground. He hadn't seen Kurt, but he had found a Big Wheel tricycle on the side of the road, and he'd brought it to the dump.

Seeing his abandoned Big Wheel, Jill immediately believed someone had taken Kurt. He was afraid of the woods, even at their home in Manchester; his sister couldn't get him to go into woods with her to play. He'd told his mother there were monsters in the woods, so she couldn't believe that he would just wander off into an unknown forest. However, the men in their group thought he may have just wandered in a little way to look for his father. The people at the campsite immediately started a search party for the little boy, and the game wardens were notified.

One of the stunning views from the campground

The wardens called in helicopters, and there was a search plane employed to help find the child. Knowing that the boy loved helicopters, wardens would fly over the woods, talking to him over the loudspeakers. They instructed Kurt to follow the helicopter and it would lead him back to his parents.

By seven that night, word had gotten back to Manchester. Ron had grown up in that town. He was a volunteer firefighter and a supervisor for the highway department. Word also reached Wayne, Maine, about thirteen miles west of Manchester, where Jill had grown up. Hearing that the Newtons' little boy was lost, people got into their vehicles and drove to the campgrounds.

Night fell and the temperature dropped to twenty-six degrees Fahrenheit. Both Ron and Jill were frantic. They refused to rest. They stood at the edge of the woods with bullhorns, calling to Kurt and listening for a response that never came. People searched throughout the night. The idea of a small, terrified little boy was driving people past the point of exhaustion.

In the morning there were 200 people searching the woods, and the authorities brought in bloodhounds to aid in finding Kurt. Unfortunately, the dogs found no trail. They only ended up circling the dump. The large numbers of people in the area may have confused the scent, or the worsening weather may have washed away whatever scent Kurt had left behind.

There were appeals on radio and television asking people to be on the lookout for Kurt, and people from all over the state came to Chain of Ponds to help. At one point, the search party swelled to 1,500 people. Nearby homes helped feed all the people who flooded the area in hopes of bringing Kurt home.

A wooded road in the campground

They even managed to get a military plane with infrared sensors, flown up from Florida, to search the woods for any signs of the boy. Jill was convinced that the plane would find Kurt, but Ron had his doubts in the technology, preferring to put his faith in the people searching the ground. Ron was one of the most dedicated searchers. He refused to rest and insisted on continuing to search for his little boy. Even when he fell and sprained his ankle and was ordered off his feet by a doctor, Ron refused to stop searching and calling for Kurt.

On Wednesday night, his friends, concerned for his health, drugged his coffee. Ron fell asleep still clutching his bullhorn. Jill was as dedicated as her husband. She flew in the helicopters, calling out to Kurt, and searched with friends on the ground.

There is over 2,000 acres of wilderness in those northern woods, and searchers did the best they could to cover every possible spot where Kurt could have been. There are caves and rocks and nooks everywhere, and it is easy to miss a spot that a small boy could curl up and hide in. Thirty-eight years later, a sixty-six-year-old woman, Geraldine Largay, would go missing on the Appalachian Trail about thirty-five miles south of where Kurt went missing. Despite having set up a campsite and surviving twenty-six days while she waited for rescue, it took wardens over two years to find Geraldine, whose campsite was less than two miles from the trail. The woods can be so dense and the terrain difficult to search that finding an entire campsite is difficult. Finding a lone child . . . nearly impossible.

The family holds out hope. They still believe that someone must have taken Kurt. As mentioned, the boy was afraid of the woods and rarely liked to leave his mother's side. So the idea of his wandering off into a wooded area seemed unlikely. Also, there was no sign of any animal having taken Kurt. If he had been attacked, there would have been evidence at the spot where his bike had been left. Abduction seems unlikely, though. The roads in this area are so rarely traveled, what are the chances that someone would come along and take a child off the road? But it's also true that it only takes the one moment of opportunity.

The Newtons had missing-child posters put up in the woods, asking outdoorsmen to report anything unusual they might see, and Ron continued to return to the woods, even bringing his snowmobile out to search the area in winter. However, since they believed that Kurt was never in the woods, they mailed out flyers to schools all across the United States, hoping that as Kurt reached school age he might be recognized as their son. They also drove all over Maine and Quebec, dropping off flyers at every store and gas station they found. They either mailed or delivered almost 75,000 posters to people across the United States and Canada.

There have been many responses to the Newtons' call for help, but to this day we don't know what happened to that little boy. I hope that someday the family will have the answers they need.

If you have any information regarding the disappearance of Kurt Newton, please contact the Maine State Police, Major Crimes Unit, at 1-800-228-0857 (in state) or (207) 657-3030 (out of state).

You can also leave an anonymous tip at their website: www.maine.gov/dps/ msp/criminal_investigation/report_crime/cid1.html

MASSACHUSETTS

THE BORDEN MURDERS

Fall River

....

IT WAS A HORRIBLE CRIME. IT WAS AN IMPOSSIBLE CRIME.
AND YET IT HAPPENED.

—HOSEA KNOWLTON, DISTRICT ATTORNEY

August 4, 1892, started as a typical day in the city of Fall River, Massachusetts; it ended with two of its prominent citizens hacked to death with a hatchet. This is, perhaps, the most infamous unsolved case in New England history.

That morning, Andrew Borden, the father and head of this small branch of the Borden clan, had a frugal breakfast with his second wife, Abby Durfee Gray Borden, and his late wife's brother, John Morse. His eldest daughter, Emma Borden, was visiting friends in Fairhaven, and his youngest daughter, Lizzie, was still upstairs. Andrew took care of a few chores, then made his way into town. He had bank business to attend to, so he left the house at about 9:00 a.m. John Morse, a surprise guest the night before, left to go visit family members on the other side of town. This left only Abby, Lizzie, and Bridget, the maid, at home.

The front door of the Borden home in Fall River

Where Abby Borden's body was found in the guest room

Abby sent Bridget outside to wash the windows, despite the sweltering heat and that Bridget, along with the rest of the household, was feeling ill. Lizzie came downstairs and was setting up in the dining room so she could iron some handkerchiefs. Abby went upstairs to clean the guest room where John had slept the previous night. Neither Lizzie nor Bridget claimed to have heard anything, but while in the guest room, Abby was brutally murdered.

Someone came up behind her and struck her nineteen times with a hatchet. Abby's body fell to the floor between the dresser and the bed, on the side farthest from the door.

This happened at about 9:30 in the morning. Andrew returned home early at about 10:30 a.m. because he too was not feeling well, but the side door, which was usually unlocked, was latched, and he could not get his key to unlock the front door, which *was* usually locked. Bridget had to let him into the house. Bridget testified that while she was struggling with the lock to let Mr. Borden in, she thought she had heard Lizzie at the top of the stairs, laughing. Andrew asked after Abby, and Lizzie told him that Abby had received a note from a sick friend, and she had gone to visit them. Andrew lay down on the couch in the sitting room, and Lizzie said that she helped him remove his boots and put on his slippers.

Lizzie then spoke to Bridget about a sale on fabric at the department store and encouraged Bridget to go. However, Bridget wasn't feeling any better, and the heat was making her feel worse. Lizzie suggested she go up to her room to take a nap, which Bridget did. Lizzie claims she went out to the barn at this time to find some lead to make sinkers for an upcoming fishing trip she was planning. Then she sat

The view of the guest bedroom from the landing, where Bridget thought she'd heard Lizzie when Andrew returned home

in the barn and ate some pears. When Lizzie came back into the house, she was met with a horrific sight. Andrew was still laid out on the couch, but now his head was split open. Someone had taken a hatchet and delivered eleven blows to Andrew's head and face. Lizzie immediately screamed for Maggie—Lizzie and Emma called Bridget by the name "Maggie" because that was their former maid's name. This was at 11:10 a.m., according to Bridget.

Lizzie sent Bridget across the street to get Dr. Bowen, who lived there. When Bridget returned to let Lizzie know that Dr. Bowen was not home, she was sent to fetch Alice Russell, Lizzie's closest friend. Mrs. Churchill, a neighbor, saw Bridget hurrying away, so she stopped to speak with Lizzie, who was standing in the doorway. Mrs. Churchill panicked on hearing that someone had murdered Andrew Borden. Frantic, she ran through the neighborhood, looking for a doctor. Another neighbor, John Cunningham, overheard the conversation and ran to Gorman's Paint Shop to call the police from their phone. This all happened within fifteen minutes of Lizzie calling out to Bridget upon finding her father's body in the sitting room.

Officer Allen received the summons and went to the Borden house to investigate the disturbance. Dr. Bowen arrived home and also went directly to the Borden house. Officer Allen, Alice Russell, and Mrs. Churchill returned to the house at approximately the same time she ran out. They found Andrew's body covered and Lizzie sitting in the kitchen.

Officer Allen checked the doors to the outside and found them all locked. He then searched all the rooms and closets on the first floor. In less than five minutes, he left a neighbor to watch over the scene while he returned to the police station to summon assistance. Dr. Bowen also left at that time to send a telegraph to Emma Borden, letting her know that her father had been murdered and that she needed to return home immediately.

The house became the center of chaos, and people were allowed inside. Neighbors, reporters, and the police wandered about the house during the investigation, making it difficult for law enforcement to find any physical evidence. In all the chaos, Lizzie asked Bridget to go upstairs, since she thought she'd heard Abby return home. However, Bridget was too scared to go anywhere in the house alone, so Mrs. Churchill accompanied her upstairs. The women found Abby's body in the spare bedroom, and the investigation was now a double homicide.

John Morse arrived back at 92 Second Street just after 11:30 that morning. He went through the gate to the back of the property, avoiding the crowd that had gathered outside the house. John then took a moment to stop and eat a couple of pears. At around 11:45 he entered the home. He was shown Andrew's and Abby's bodies, and then he stopped to chat with Lizzie. John then spent the rest of the afternoon in the backyard.

Lizzie went to her room to rest, but before she could lie down, Assistant Marshal Fleet and Reverend Buck questioned her. This is the interview in which Lizzie famously corrected her interrogator: "She's not my mother; she's my stepmother."

The spot where Andrew Borden was murdered

The police searched the house, including the basement, where they found several hatchets—one with a missing handle that the police found particularly interesting.

All this time, people were coming and going while the bodies lay where they were slain. It wasn't until three in the afternoon that the photographer arrived to take the crime scene photos. Once that was done, Andrew's and Abby's bodies were removed from the home and brought to the undertaker, James Winward.

At around 5:00 p.m., Emma Borden arrived back in Fall River, immediately returning to the house to be with Lizzie. That night the police kept a watch on the house and observed Lizzie going down to the basement twice—once with Alice Russell and once alone. It has been speculated that Lizzie could have gone down to wash out any bloody clothes in the laundry, but no one has been able to prove what she was doing down there. Plus, Alice Russell would have informed police if anything questionable had happened.

There were other possible suspects. People reported seeing a strange "smelly" man walking on Second Street between the time of Abby's and Andrew's murders. He was about five feet, four inches tall with dark hair and a pale face. Not only was he seen by several residents of Second Street, including Bridget, but also by a Fall River police officer, who saw a man of this description. It was believed that he must have been one of the Portuguese immigrants who had moved into the area. The Portuguese were the current group of immigrants who were the first to be suspected of any wrongdoing, having recently replaced the Irish in that category. However, nothing ever came of that possible lead.

Bridget was also an early suspect since she was at the house when both murders occurred. Plus, she was Irish, having moved to the United States in 1887, so she fell under anti-immigrant prejudices. This meant that she was suspected of knowing more than she was telling. She likely wasn't the killer, however, since she had been outside washing windows at the time of Abby's death and was napping in her bedroom on the third floor when Andrew was killed.

Emma Borden was never considered because she had been out of town all that week. Therefore, it wasn't likely she had snuck into Fall River, killed Abby and Andrew, and gotten back to Fairhaven in time to receive the telegraph from Dr. Bowen to return home. Even if she'd had the time, no one saw her traveling between the two cities.

John Morse was also questioned by the police, but he had an alibi, an incredibly detailed alibi. John had been visiting other family members, and he was with them at the times of the murders. The odd thing about John's alibi, though, was the mundane details he remembered from that day. He took a streetcar back to the Borden home and was able to provide the name of the car's conductor, the street car's number, and detailed descriptions of the passengers in the car. These are not details one would usually pay attention to on an average day. More like someone looking to be sure they had witnesses to corroborate an alibi. It was also strange that John claimed he didn't notice the large crowd outside the house or the police on the property when he was snacking on pears in the backyard before entering the house. John Morse's behavior was notably strange.

The police, however, almost immediately had their prime suspect: Lizzie. She was suspected because of her strange attitude after the murders and her conflicting stories. Also, she had told people that Abby had received a note and had left, when actually, Abby had never left the house, and the note from a sick friend was never found. No one ever came forward as the author of such a note. Emma and Lizzie offered a $5,000 reward if someone came forward with information about the author of the note or any information that led to an arrest of Andrew's and Abby's killer(s). Both Emma and Lizzie had a strained relationship with their stepmother, and Andrew was infamous for being stingy—leaving his daughters living in cramped quarters and in fear of being left penniless if Andrew died, leaving his money to Abby instead of them. In fact, there was a rumor that Andrew had plans to do just that, but it was never proven. Things were so tense in the Borden household that the sisters ate their meals at a separate time from Abby and Andrew—presumably to avoid being around the couple.

The police's suspicion of Lizzie was only increased when they found out that she had burned a dress in the kitchen stove. Lizzie claimed the dress had been hanging in the pantry and was going to be thrown out because there were paint stains on it. A seamstress confirmed that she had fitted Lizzie for a dress that had been stained with paint weeks earlier. Whether an innocent mistake or a deliberate attempt to hide evidence, it didn't look good for Lizzie.

On August 6, the same day as the funeral, the police conducted another search of the home. They confiscated the hatchets seen in the basement on the day of the murder and searched through Emma's and Lizzie's clothes. That evening the mayor and a police officer stopped by the house to speak with the sisters, and during this

The Borden family monument in Fall River's Oak Grove Cemetery

conversation they confirmed that Lizzie was an official suspect.

On August 9, Lizzie was required to appear at an inquest. Her request that her lawyer, Andrew Jennings, accompany her was denied. Lizzie didn't do well on the stand. She often contradicted herself and was often confused by the questions. Her attitude seemed so poor to prosecuting lawyer Hosea Knowlton that he became quite brutal and brought her to tears by being too specific about the details of Andrew's death and his condition when she'd found him. Unfortunately for Knowlton, because Lizzie had been told she was a suspect, she should have been allowed a lawyer, and nothing she said at the inquest could be used at trial.

Much has been made of Lizzie's inability to keep her story straight, and her detached manner for much of the investigation. There is an explanation for Lizzie's odd behavior: morphine. From the morning of the murders, Dr. Bowen had been giving Lizzie regular doses of morphine to help calm her nerves. This could explain her erratic behavior and her confused testimony, although this was not a factor in the inquest. At its end, on August 11, police arrested Lizzie and put her in jail.

Lizzie's trial started on June 5, 1893. It was a media sensation and was called the trial of the century. Lizzie had her "Dream Team" representing her: her family's lawyer, Andrew Jennings; Melvin Adams, the future US attorney for the District of Massachusetts; and George Robinson, a former governor of Massachusetts. Hosea Knowlton, future attorney general of Massachusetts, was the prosecutor.

Both sides had a lot to overcome. The defense had to deal with explaining why Lizzie had burned a dress only the day after she found out she was the suspect in the murder. There was also the missing note. The fact that despite the reward of $5,000, no one had come forward to say they had either sent or delivered that note, didn't look good for Lizzie. Also, if the murderer wasn't a member of the household, a stranger was in the home for several hours without being discovered, or managed to gain entry twice without being noticed. Both scenarios seemed dubious.

As mentioned, the prosecution was unable to use any of the testimony from the inquest, because Lizzie should have been allowed her lawyer since she was a suspect in the murder. The evidence that Lizzie tried to buy prussic acid the day before the murders was not allowed by Judge William Moody. He felt it was not relevant to the crime, since it happened the day before, and too much time had passed for it to be connected. The hatchets found in the basement could not be conclusively linked to the wounds on the victims. Also, the chaos of the scene led to conflicting reports from the police (one officer claimed that the handle for the broken hatchet was nearby, while another stated that the handle was gone).

On June 20, after fifteen days of courtroom drama, the jury began their deliberations. It took the twelve men less than two hours to come back with a verdict of not guilty. Lizzie was acquitted and free to go home. However, Lizzie was cleared only by the legal system. The people of Fall River were not so forgiving. While they supported her innocence during the trial, it became clear afterward that they only wanted to avoid the public scandal of a rich white woman being convicted of killing her parents right in the heart of their city. No, they released Lizzie back into Fall River society, but she was not accepted into it.

She was not welcomed back to any of the organizations where she had previously volunteered, and the press hounded her. Then there is this quaint little rhyme:

Lizzie Borden took an axe
And gave her mother forty whacks.
When she saw what she had done,
She gave her father forty-one.

Children chanted that while they played in the neighborhood.

If Lizzie thought that moving to the upscale part of Fall River would spare her the schoolyard taunts, she was wrong. Emma and Lizzie moved to the posh Fall River neighborhood called "the Hill." They bought a home, named it "Maplecroft," hired servants, and lived at a much-higher standard than they had at their old home on Second Street. Lizzie changed her name to Lizbeth and found a new society that

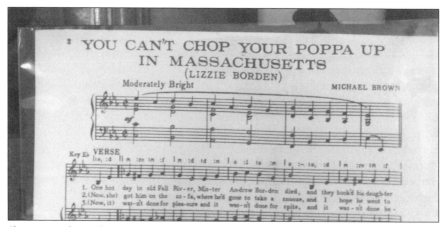

Sheet music of a novelty song in the Bordens' sitting room

she could socialize with. Lizbeth befriended many actors and hosted parties at her new home. People considered it quite scandalous since at this time actors were still considered "lowlifes." Lizbeth was especially close to actress Nance O'Neil. Emma Borden, who had moved to Maplecroft with Lizbeth, did not approve of the parties, which were frequent in the home. She did not approve of the quality of people that Lizbeth was socializing with and bringing into their home. In 1904, Emma moved out of the house, and the sisters never saw each other again.

Lizbeth lived in Fall River for the rest of her life, and other than once being accused of shoplifting in 1897, she was not in trouble with the law again. She remained a pariah of Fall River society, but she never moved away. Lizzie died on June 1, 1927, of pneumonia. No one else has ever been tried for the murders of Andrew and Abby Borden.

Theories

After 125 years, there are hundreds of theories. It seems like no one who ever met the Bordens is above suspicion. Andrew Borden was a taciturn businessman and had many people whom he had alienated with his business. So most people who worked with or for him could have had a motive.

Of course, Lizzie is still most people's choice. She was one of two people who we know were at the house at the time of both murders, Bridget being the other. As for motive, at first, people believed she may have killed Andrew and Abby for money. As stated above, people believed that there was a possibility that Andrew was planning on changing the will to favor Abby and to cut out Emma and Lizzie. There was also the frugal way in which Andrew maintained the house. There was no flush toilet or electric lights, and the house was small and cramped. Lizzie wanted a grander lifestyle than her father was willing to provide.

Much later, minds turned to thinking that Andrew may have been sexually abusing his daughters, and that Lizzie, with or without conspirators, killed Andrew to end the abuse. There are also allegations that Abby caught Lizzie in a lesbian tryst and that Lizzie killed Abby and Andrew to keep her secret. There is no evidence to suggest abuse on the part of either Abby or Andrew, either at the time or in any documents that researchers have found since. Admittedly, such things were rarely discussed at that time, but if that were the case you'd think that there might be some inference to it in all the documents and correspondence. As for Lizzie killing to keep her sexuality a secret, it is possible, but again there is no proof. There were rumors about Lizzie being a lesbian, but that does not prove anything. Again, we don't know.

Another theory is that Bridget killed the Bordens. Angry at Mrs. Borden for making her go outside and wash the windows in the blistering heat while she was ill, Bridget snapped and killed Mrs. Borden. Then she took her ire out on Mr. Borden when he arrived home. However, why would she leave Lizzie alive? Yes, Mrs. Borden had given Bridget an unpleasant job to do, but both Lizzie and Emma refused to call Bridget by her name. They called her Maggie because that was the

The graves of the older generation of Bordens

name of their previous maid, and I can't see sparing the person who can't even get your name right if you are going on a killing spree ... unless she hoped that Lizzie would be convicted in her place, but then wouldn't she have done more to implicate Lizzie in her testimony?

There is also a theory that Bridget was Lizzie's lover, and they killed the Bordens together to keep their secret. Again, there is nothing to prove this, and if they killed Abby and Andrew to keep their secret, why did they not stay together afterward?

John Morse is a favorite suspect too. Lizzie did testify that she heard John and her father have a heated discussion on the night before the murder, and John and Andrew did have business deals together, so there could have been a motive there. John's behavior on the day of the murder and his overly detailed alibi makes him seems suspicious, but he did have an alibi for at least the time of Andrew's murder. However, he would have had time to kill Abby if he'd left the house immediately after killing her.

In Arnold Brown's book *Lizzie Borden: The Legend, the Truth, the Final Chapter*, he speculates that Andrew had an illegitimate son, William Borden, and that William was an unstable and angry man who was in Fall River that day to confront his father and demand either recognition as his son or money. When things did not go his way, William snapped and killed Abby, then waited for Andrew to return home, when William killed him as well. However, there is no record or rumor at that time that any of this was going on. Again, this isn't something that could be kept mostly quiet, but once Andrew was gone, any of these secrets would have been widely discussed if there was any hint. People do love scandals.

I don't think Lizzie killed Abby and Andrew. Maybe she was an innocent bystander, but more likely she was aware of what happened and didn't reveal the real killer. Unless some new evidence comes to light, this will remain one of New England's most infamous unsolved mysteries.

THE GREAT PLYMOUTH MAIL TRUCK ROBBERY

ALTHOUGH THE WORLD HAS ALWAYS BEEN GARNISHED
WITH BOODLE AND SALTED WITH THIEVES, THE ODDS
AGAINST A MAN SATISFYING HIS DREAMS OF AVARICE BY
MEANS OF ARMED ROBBERY HAVE BEEN LAMENTABLY HIGH
SINCE THE BEGINNING OF TIME.

—PAUL O'NEIL

It was late in the afternoon on August 14, 1962, when Patrick Schena and William Barrett left Boston. They were going to pick up registered-currency pouches from the Hyannis and Buzzard's Bay post offices, then return them to Boston. They completed the pickups with no problems. However, their cargo would not make it to the Federal Reserve Bank in Boston.

Just after the two men passed exit 3 on Route 3 in Plymouth, a man dressed as a highway worker rerouted traffic. He set it up so that all traffic was forced to use exit 3 onto Clark Road. He even stopped a tourist who missed the sign and almost drove past the detour.

However, Patrick and William were unaware of what was happening behind them. Patrick told reporters that a car passed him going about 80 mph, but there was no other traffic in the northbound lane. Not long after being passed, Patrick saw two cars on the side of the road, and as the mail truck approached, a police officer stepped into the road to wave them over. When they stopped, the two vehicles pulled out to block them from driving anywhere. The truck was then rushed by two men with machine guns (some reports indicated they had shotguns).

Patrick and William were disarmed and forced into the back of the truck, where they were bound and gagged. The robbers drove them around and made several stops to drop off money. According to *Life Magazine*, the two robbers were Tony, dressed as a police officer, and Buster, the guy who drove the mail truck to the drop-off points. The robbers would drive for a while, stop, and then Tony would hand a couple of the money bags to Buster, who would, most likely, drop them off to an accomplice. This went on for about an hour and a half. When Tony

The Plymouth Post Office

and Buster had finished unloading the sixteen bags of cash, Buster drove the truck around for about twenty minutes, then parked it on the side of Route 128. Tony threatened Patrick and William, "Lie still or you're dead! Don't move for ten minutes," and then left. The men waited in the back of the mail truck for a moment, then Patrick stood up and tried to get to the front of the truck. Tony slid the side door open and threatened to blow Patrick's head off. Patrick lay back down and waited for a few more minutes—he didn't want anyone to shoot him in the head, but he got back up. This time there was no one there to stop him.

He hopped out of the truck and tried to wave down a passing vehicle. The only person who would stop for him was Ricardo G. Unde-Freire, a premed student from Ecuador. Patrick informed Ricardo of what happened, and asked him to get help. Ricardo, riding a moped, drove off as fast as he could. He eventually came across a pay phone and tried to report the crime. The police did not believe him, and he had to drive to Stoughton, where he managed to find a cop on the street. He was actually taken to the station and questioned. It took awhile, but he finally got the police to believe him, and they set up roadblocks despite not knowing who or what to look for. The thieves had gotten away with $1.5 million (approximately $12.5 million in 2018 dollars).

The next morning, the postal inspectors and the FBI were investigating the case, but there was very little useful information. There was a lot coming in, but it was all hysteria driven—hysteria and media hype plus a hefty reward for the recovery of the stolen money. The FBI offered 10 percent of the money recovered, with $50,000 added by the postmaster general; this led to wild speculation and more than one person being falsely accused of the crime.

Plymouth, Massachusetts

The media did not help matters; they proclaimed people guilty without any evidence and added to the circus-like atmosphere. *Life Magazine* went down to Plymouth to work the story and did a reenactment without notifying local law enforcement. On top of that, the article in *Life* was irreverent. They were in awe of the thieves, referring to the heist as "a pleasant crime and one with literary overtones" and "They had behaved with imagination and intelligence, they had spilled no blood, they had enlivened the dreary lives of multitudes and had, in one sense, contrived to steal an enormous sum of money without really costing anyone a nickel." They even imagined the "jolly scene" when the gang was reunited. Police estimated that six people were involved in the robbery. The author of the piece, Paul O'Neil, does concede that there may be dissent among the group about how to split their windfall, but his biggest concern is "If they do not get caught, how in the name of Alcatraz are any of us going to find out what really happened?"

Admittedly, at the time of this article the robbery was fairly harmless, other than traumatizing the two postal workers and creating a $1.5 million loss to be divided by the twelve Federal Reserve banks whose money was being transported. The money stolen, according to O'Neil, was less than the cost of insurance that the banks had stopped carrying to save money. Sadly, this "victimless" crime would not stay bloodless.

In the first few days after the robbery, law enforcement was confident they would capture the robbers in no time. However, as days, weeks, months, and years passed, the pressure to solve this was getting overwhelming. As the statute of limitations approached, the postal inspectors and Department of Justice were putting huge amounts of pressure on anyone with a criminal history. They were especially focused on anyone with a history of robbery.

In 1967, the police believed they had found the culprits. A tip from a prison inmate led them to three people: two men and a woman—Thomas R. Richards of Weymouth, John J. Kelley of Watertown, and Patricia J. Diaferio of Roslindale. In the summer of 1967, a grand jury indicted the three. Thomas Richards was the driver, and he turned informant against his two colleagues. However, Thomas would never get his day in court. He was last seen several days before he was to testify, but he did not show up for court. In *Beyond Plymouth Rock: America's Hometown in the 20th Century*, Grace Begley states, "At least fifteen other suspects or informants on the case were murdered or disappeared." She also tells about the intimidation tactics used against those working the case. Her father was a postal inspector, and a member of the robbery gang tailed him around town. At night, while the family slept, her armed father would also patrol their home.

Now far gone from the "victimless" crime glorified by *Life Magazine* five years earlier, the body count was likely in the double digits. The suspects were holding much of the area in fear, and it worked. With Thomas Richards either having run off or dead, there was no way to prove that either John Kelly or Patricia Diaferio had anything to do with the crime, and the court acquitted them. No one else can be charged with the crime, since the statute of limitations ended in 1967. So we will never know "who done it," and Paul O'Neil, who died in 1988, never got his salacious details of the crime.

ISABELLA STEWART GARDNER MUSEUM

Boston

....

IMAGINE IF YOU COULD NEVER HEAR BEETHOVEN'S
SEVENTH SYMPHONY AGAIN, EVER. WELL, A VERMEER IS
CERTAINLY AT THAT LEVEL OF CREATION, AND SO IS THE
STORM OF THE SEA OF GALILEE.

—ANNE HAWLEY, ISABELLA STEWART GARDNER

MUSEUM DIRECTOR (1989–2015)

Isabella Stewart Gardner was as close to Boston royalty as we've gotten. She was the ultimate rich, eccentric Bostonian. Ironically, though, she wasn't born in Boston. Isabella Stewart was born on April 14, 1840, in New York City into a wealthy merchant family. She lived in New York until she was sixteen; then her family moved to Paris, France, where her parents enrolled Isabella in a school for American girls. She was able to travel to Italy at this time, and she developed a fondness for Italian art and architecture. In 1858, she returned to America, and shortly after her return, she was invited to visit a former classmate, Julia Gardner, in Boston. Here she met and fell in love with Julia's brother, John "Jack" Gardner Jr. They were married on April 10, 1860, in New York City, then moved to Boston, where they lived the rest of their lives. They settled happily in Boston, and, in June 1863, they welcomed their son, John "Jackie" Gardner III, into the world. Sadly, young Jackie died of pneumonia when he was only two years old. Naturally, Isabella was devastated by Jack's death and the miscarriage she suffered the year after his death.

To help alleviate her depression and post-miscarriage illness, Jack took her on a tour of Europe. This trip did help to improve her spirits and started Isabella on her passion for collecting art. While Isabella and Jack never had any more children of their own, in 1875 Jack's brother, Joseph, died and the couple took in his three sons and raised them.

The courtyard of the Isabella Stewart Gardner Museum. Every room in the old section on the museum is open to the courtyard, allowing visitors to be able to enjoy the scent of that season's flowers wafting through the building.

November's chrysanthemums add a splash of color to the stairs leading to the Dutch Room on the second floor.

Jack and Isabella traveled often to exotic locations all over the world, and they were always looking for new, interesting pieces to add to their collection. When at home in Boston, they often had parties. Their guest lists usually included artists, writers, and musicians instead of members of high society.

Isabella didn't conform to the expected behavior of a member of Boston society. In fact, she delighted in shocking the "bluebloods" that she did keep company with. One story tells of Isabella almost causing a riot at a symphony in 1912. She was a huge fan of the city's baseball team, the Boston Red Sox (she is such a noted fan that the museum will take $2 off the price of admission if you are wearing any Red Sox gear), and that year they had won the World Series. So that December, she celebrated by wearing a white headband with "Oh you Red Sox" written on it in red. This caused such a commotion that people say even the musicians were distracted from their sheet music. The symphony crowd was not only taken aback by her strange apparel, but that it referenced a song that was popular with "the Royal Rooters," an infamous drunken and rowdy group of fans. Perhaps they feared she was going to burst out into bawdy song or tip over a piano. Isabella did seem to love tweaking the noses of Boston's high society, and this seemingly harmless gesture was quite a shock for them.

After Jack died in 1898, Isabella started serious work on building a museum to house their collections. She purchased land in the Fenway area of Boston and started building a Venetian-style palace. The museum centered on an indoor courtyard. All three floors surrounded the courtyard and had windows that were opened to it, allowing the smell of the garden to permeate the air throughout. The fourth floor was of the same design but was set aside as living quarters for Isabella, which are now used as offices for museum staff.

Isabella had a hand in all aspects of the museum, from the design of the building to the placement of the art, and to the men she worked with, she was notoriously stubborn and opinionated. Her collection is varied, containing not only paintings and sculpture but also correspondence of historical interest, tapestries, flags, and furniture. It is a perfect mixture to represent her eclectic aesthetic.

What was the front of the Gardner Museum at the time of the robbery, as seen from Fenway (the road, not the stadium)

The museum opened to the public in 1903, and Isabella curated her collection until her death on July 17, 1924. She had created a $1 million endowment for the museum but stipulated that there can be no alteration to the permanent collection. So the museum will remain as she had envisioned it.

Theft

On March 18, 1990, while the city of Boston was still celebrating Saint Patrick's Day, two men sat waiting in a car. There were occasional partygoers straggling by their vehicle. Then, at 1:24 a.m., the two approached the door to the museum. Twenty-three-year-old night watchman Richard Abath had returned from his rounds of the museum when he saw two men in police uniforms approach. They rang the buzzer and told Richard that there had been a disturbance reported, and he needed to let them into the museum to investigate.

This is when Richard made a $500 million mistake. He buzzed them in—despite a museum policy that no one was to be allowed access to the museum during night hours without a supervisor's permission. Once they had gained entrance to the building and approached the security desk, one of the officers claimed to recognize Richard as someone who had outstanding warrants. Richard assumed it was a case of mistaken identity that would be quickly cleared up. It wasn't until after they had lured him away from the desk, where the alarm was located, and handcuffed him that Richard realized something was wrong. They hadn't frisked him, and when he looked closer at the mustache on one "officer," he noticed it was fake. When the other guard arrived, he was subdued, and both guards were then tied up with duct tape, handcuffed, and left in the basement.

After this, the two robbers spent the next eighty-one minutes robbing the museum. We know their movements that night from the motion detectors installed there. From the basement, they went straight to the second floor's "Dutch Room," where they tried to steal Rembrandt's *Self Portrait, Age 23*, but they were unable to remove it from the frame. So they focused on cutting Rembrandt's *The Storm on the Sea of Galilee* and *A Lady and Gentleman in Black* out of their frames. They continued through the museum, taking thirteen works of art and making two trips from the museum to their car (see list of stolen works that follows). The robbers then drove off and have never been found. The two guards were left in the basement until the day crew came in and began to search for them.

Johannes Vermeer's *The Concert* was painted in 1664 and was 28.5 by 25.5 inches. The installation of this oil-on-canvas painting included a chair and desk so that patrons could sit and enjoy it. Its frame was broken in the robbery. It depicts three musicians, a vocalist, a harpsichord player, and a lute player, performing. This is one of only thirty-six known paintings by Vermeer, and according to the museum's website, it was the most valuable painting stolen and may be the most valuable stolen object in the world.

Several Rembrandt pieces were taken that night:

A Lady and Gentleman in Black was painted in 1633 and is 51.8 by 43 inches. It was hanging on the wall in the Dutch Room and was cut from its frame with box cutters. This painting is oil on canvas. It is a portrait of a quiet and refined husband and wife.

The Storm on the Sea of Galilee was painted in 1633 and is 64 by 50.4 inches. This oil-on-canvas painting is the only seascape painted by Rembrandt. It was in the Dutch Room and cut from its frame with box cutters.

Rembrandt's Self Portrait was a framed self-portrait etched in ink, and it is barely bigger than a postage stamp.

Landscape with an Obelisk was painted in 1638 by Govaert Flinck and is 21.5 by 28 inches. This oil-on-wood painting was thought to be by Rembrandt, but in the 1970s it was recognized as the work of Flinck, his pupil. It was on the opposite side of The Concert as part of the desktop display. It was also broken out of its frame, and police believe this may have been mistaken for another Rembrandt painting by the thieves.

The front entryway to the museum at the time of the robbery

The courtyard of the Isabella Stewart Gardner Museum. At the time of the robbery, the main entrance would have been just to the left of this picture, and the stairs to the second floor directly behind the photographer.

A Shang-dynasty Chinese bronze beaker, gu, from the twelfth century BCE was also taken from a display in the Dutch Room. It was displayed on a table next to The Storm on the Sea of Galilee.

Five works of Edgar Degas were taken from displays in the Short Gallery. La Sortie du Pelage is a pencil and watercolor on paper.

Cortege aux Environs de Florence is pencil and wash on paper.

Three Mounted Jockeys is oil on brown paper.

The Program for an Artistic Soiree is charcoal on white paper.

The Program for an Artistic Soiree is charcoal on buff paper.

Édouard Manet's Chez Tortoni was painted between 1879 and 1880 and is 10 by 13 inches. This oil on canvas is the only item to go missing from the Blue Room, and the painting's frame was found on the security chief's chair, near the front desk. Its theft has led to suspicions about Richard Abath's involvement in the robbery ever since; according to motion detectors, he was the only person to enter the Blue Room on the night of the robbery.

Napoleonic Eagle Finial. The framed flag is the standard of Napoleon's Imperial Guard.

Why Steal Art?

Art is one of the most difficult items for thieves to fence. Stealing the pieces can be easy, since many museums are notoriously lax in security (finding a way to properly display and protect these objects isn't difficult). So, stealing a piece can be as easy as grabbing it and walking out of the building. There have been instances where that has happened or of a security guard chasing and tackling a thief as they run out into the street. However, once the art has been taken can be where things get really tricky. Unlike money, which is usually easy to pass on, or jewelry that can be broken down and the parts sold off, a painting's or sculpture's value often rests on its identity. So you can't sell a Degas or a Rembrandt without identifying what it is. Therefore, unless you have a buyer lined up in advance, it is going to be difficult to sell, and if it does sell, it is for a small fraction of the actual value of the piece.

There are benefits to stealing art. Myles Connor discusses two reasons in his book The Art of the Heist. First is the thrill. Getting away with something can be exhilarating even if you don't profit from it monetarily. The second reason to steal art is that it can be used as a bargaining chip with law enforcement to either drop charges against someone or lighten a jail sentence. Connor tells the story of stealing

The side door for the museum, where Richard Abath stepped out for a moment on the night of the robbery

a painting from Boston's Museum of Fine Art, then returning it to authorities in exchange for dropping the charges against him in a different case.

Connor is not a suspect in the Gardner Museum theft because he was in federal prison at the time of the robbery. He claims to have no idea where the paintings are, but he is searching for them—only partially because of the offered reward.

Theories

I've heard people say that anyone in New England in the 1990s and after has been a suspect in either the theft or having been involved or complicit in hiding the stolen artwork.

As mentioned earlier, authorities have suspected Richard Abath since the time of the theft. He is the person who let the robbers into the museum and also behaved suspiciously the night of the robbery. He opened the side door that led to Palace Road at the end of his rounds that evening. Was this a signal to the thieves that he was going to be back at the desk to let them in? He is also the only person who was in the Blue Room, where *Chez Tortoni* was taken from. Did he stash it away somewhere to keep for himself, or for the robbers to grab without having to go into that part of the museum? Abath has maintained his innocence and he has lived a modest lifestyle, so he doesn't appear to have gained monetarily from the robbery. Although Abath was a struggling musician who liked to party, some have suggested he may have helped the robbers in exchange for paying off any debts he might have had.

There was no shortage of criminal element in Boston, and according to Stephen Kurkjian's book *Master Thieves: The Boston Gangsters Who Pulled Off the World's Greatest Art Heist*, the museum was known to be an easy target in Boston's criminal underworld. One just needs to figure out which of those very colorful characters actually pulled off the heist. The FBI now reports that they know who the thieves were, but the bureau isn't releasing the information, and that they are on the verge of finding the paintings and the person holding them. That was in August 2015. The FBI has said that the two men they believe did the actual robbery are dead, but they are closing in on the person hiding the paintings.

At of the writing of this book, it appears that their main suspect is Robert "Bobby the Cook" Gentile, described as a gangster from Hartford, Connecticut. Gentile allegedly received the paintings sometime in the early 2000s from a mobster named Robert Guarente. At this time, Gentile is being charged with possession of illegal guns, probably in hopes that he will reveal the location of the missing artwork. As of early 2017, he has not provided this information, and the eighty-year-old is claiming that he is being framed by the FBI.

No one can be charged with the theft at the Isabella Stewart Gardner Museum, since the statute of limitations is five years and the paintings were stolen twenty-seven years ago. The FBI has also said they will not charge anyone with receiving stolen goods if they turn the paintings in to authorities. The fact that no one has turned in the artwork is troubling.

New Hampshire

BEAR BROOK MURDERS

Allenstown

HOW COULD SOMEONE DO WHAT WAS DONE,
AND THOSE FOUR ANGELS WAVED GOODBYE TO NO ONE.
TALK ABOUT HEARTACHE AND DISASTER
MORE THAN ONE CAN EXPLAIN,
FOUR ANGELS WENT OFF TO HEAVEN ALONE
AND NOBODY KNEW THEIR NAME.

—DENISE

(PART OF POEM POSTED ON HTTP://OAKHILLRESEARCH.BLOGSPOT.COM)

One constant besides death and taxes in this life is hunting season, at least in New England. I know in my family that those few autumn weeks of the year meant that we would rarely see my father and brothers during daylight hours. They spent every spare moment in the woods hunting for bird and deer, and it is that way for many families in rural areas. The woods ring with gunshots and everyone starts wearing safety orange.

It is the same in Allenstown, New Hampshire. So on November 10, 1985, it was not an odd sight to see a man spending his Sunday walking in the woods near Bear Brook State Park—searching for that good spot where he was sure to "bag his deer." However, on this Sunday he found something terrible. On the side of a wooded trail just off Edgewood Drive, he stumbled across an overturned fifty-five-gallon metal oil drum. Nothing unusual there; however, when he saw the two bodies in the drum, that was what would stay with this hunter. He quickly notified the police, who were only able to tell that the remains were of an adult female and a young girl. They both had died of blunt-force trauma; their bodies were then dismembered, wrapped in plastic, and stuffed inside the metal barrel.

More details came later. The woman was five feet two to five feet seven tall, with wavy or curly brown hair. She was twenty-two to thirty-three years old and had a mix of white and Native American ancestry. She'd had a lot of dental work done; three of her teeth had been extracted, and she had many fillings. The girl was between five and eleven years old. She was probably four feet three to four feet six tall, with light-brown to dark-blonde hair. She had no fillings, but there was a gap in her front teeth. There were also signs in the girl's lungs that she suffered from pneumonia. Authorities estimated that the two had been dead since sometime between 1978 and 1984.

To complicate things, one day after the hunter discovered the bodies, another murder took place. This case was a higher priority for the police, since it was a more immediate crime and more likely to have a resolution. Danny Paquette was murdered in a field in Hookset, New Hampshire. At first it was thought to be a hunting accident, but police soon realized that this was murder. The case went unsolved until 2004, when Paquette's stepdaughter revealed that a classmate, Eric Windhurst, had killed her stepfather to protect her from his abuse. So, at the time of discovering the bodies, the police focused on the Paquette slaying. However, they still did what they could to identify the victims found near Bear Brook State Park.

But the police were getting nowhere, and the people of Allenstown were left with nothing but fear. Not only was the killer unknown, but so were the victims. The people of the area raised money to have a gravestone set up for the two victims, but it shows no names, and since they are needed for forensic evidence, no bodies rest beneath. Everything about this case is unknown. The police searched for any missing-persons reports throughout the United States and Canada, but there was no clear match, and the case went cold.

On May 9, 2000, New Hampshire State Police Sergeant John Cody was on a break between cases and decided to look at this cold case. While checking the area where the bodies had been dumped, Sgt. Cody saw more metal oil barrels, similar to the one found fifteen years before. To his shock, he found two more bodies in one of the barrels. This time it was two young girls, again wrapped in plastic and stuffed into the barrel. He was only 300 yards away from where the first two bodies had been found.

Police determined that these girls were killed at about the same time as the woman and girl found in 1985. They had most likely been left in the woods at the same time. The first of these little Jane Does was between two and four years old, three feet three to three feet nine tall, with brown hair, and she also had a gap in her front teeth, with a noticeable overbite. The second child found in 2000 was one to three years old and about two feet one to two feet six tall. She had light-brown hair and, like the other two children, had a gap in her front teeth.

This was unthinkable. Four people had gone missing at the same time and no one had noticed! It only got more baffling in 2013, when locals raised money to do DNA testing on the bodies. The results came back that the woman was maternally related to the oldest and youngest child. She was either their mother, sister, or aunt. The middle girl is not maternally related to the others.

Then in November 2015, the National Center for Missing and Exploited Children (NCMEC) had new reconstructions done, and the state's attorney general held a press conference with more information they had gleaned about the woman

A lonely road near the woods close to Bear Brook State Park

Tall trees surrounding a clearing in the park

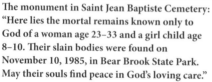

The monument in Saint Jean Baptiste Cemetery: "Here lies the mortal remains known only to God of a woman age 23–33 and a girl child age 8–10. Their slain bodies were found on November 10, 1985, in Bear Brook State Park. May their souls find peace in God's loving care."

Small waterway in the park

and girls. The woman was likely the mother of the two girls, and all four of them had been living together in the Northeast (probably in the immediate area) for two weeks to three months before they died. The woman and her likely daughters were from the area, but it appears that the middle child had come from the Dakotas or Nebraska. This is information based on testing done to the hair and teeth of all four people.

The hunt for the identity of the Allenstown Four, as locals call them, is still active. Carol Schweitzer of NCMEC is working with the New Hampshire State Police to get the information out. In a video released by NCMEC, she states: "We have never, actually, seen four unidentified bodies found together that remain unidentified after all these years." NEMEC has created new images of what they believe the woman and children would have looked like, and these photos are being distributed. They believe there must be someone out there still alive who knows these four people.

It isn't only law enforcement that is looking for their identities. Ronda Randall and her brother, Scott Maxwell, started Oakhill Research, and they have focused their efforts on locating people who were living in Bear Brook Gardens, the trailer park near where the bodies were found, at the time. Their blog, http://

Reconstruction of victims by CarlK90245. Courtesy of Wikimedia Commons by permission

oakhillresearch.blogspot.com, has information and detailed maps of the area. This is no easy task, since the park had a reputation. It was a stopping-off place for convicts recently released from jail, and at least one person who lived in the park at the estimated time of the murder was a convicted sex offender.

The people of Allenstown are now forced to confront the dark nature of humanity, since when looking to solve a case like this, so many secrets come out, and there have been so many suspects. It must be hard to look at anyone in your neighborhood and not suspect them of something dark.

Authorities are hopeful that someone will be able to identify the Allenstown Four, and once they are, perhaps, their killer can be brought to justice as well.

‖‖‖

Update:

During the writing of this book, one of the girls has been identified. DNA tests matched the unrelated girl to Bob Evans, who had been in jail for the murder of Eunsoon Jun, a chemist from California. She married Evans in 2002, and he beat her to death and dismembered her not long after. The court sentenced Evans to fifteen years for Jun's death.

Evans is also suspected in the presumed murder of a Manchester, New Hampshire, woman, Denise Beaudin. In 1981, they were traveling to California from New Hampshire, but Denise never made it. Evans kept Denise's daughter for a few years before dropping her off in a California RV park in 1986. The girl was adopted, and reports state that she is doing well.

So, one of the little girls found in the woods was Evans's daughter. Therefore, police theorize that he was the person who killed the four. (It would be a stunning coincidence that the daughter of a convicted killer was murdered by a different person.) Unfortunately, police can't interview Bob Evans because he died in prison in 2010. It is hoped, though, that this information will give us clues about who the others are, and if there is any evidence that Evans is the killer.

If you have any information about the case, contact the New Hampshire State Police Major Crimes Unit, either Detective John Sonia or Captain Mark Myrdek, at 1-603-271-2663, or call the National Center for Missing and Exploited Children at 1-800 THE LOST.

THE CONNECTICUT RIVER VALLEY KILLER

Vermont and New Hampshire

Wooded area near where Cathy Millican's body was found

The Connecticut River valley's wooded borderland between New Hampshire and Vermont, also known as the "Upper Valley" is a beautiful area—paradise for outdoorsmen and with ready access to hiking, boating, hunting, fishing, and skiing. Sadly, someone used their knowledge of the Upper Valley's wilderness areas to hunt and kill women and leave their bodies in the woods, where their remains could lie abandoned for years.

Cathy Millican is the first known victim of this killer. On October 24, 1978, Cathy drove to the Chandler Wetland Preserve in New London, New Hampshire. Someone told her that they had seen some ducks at the preserve, and since they were a rare breed not usually seen in the area, Cathy, an avid birdwatcher, rushed off that evening. She never returned home. She was reported missing the following day, and a police officer remembered seeing her Volkswagen Rabbit in the preserve's parking lot the previous evening. Searchers found her body, partly covered in brush, between one of the paths and the highway. They found her possessions scattered around the preserve's path. The police theorize that the killer had waited for her near the entry to the preserve, since he knew Cathy would need to walk past. He then attacked her as she tried to leave the preserve. He dragged and carried her along the trails to the spot where he killed her, and then took her to the area where

Path near where Cathy Millican was murdered on October 24, 1978

her body was found. The detectives on the case believed that as the police cruiser drove through the parking lot that evening, Cathy Millican's killer had been waiting, out of sight, for her to try to get back to her car.

For three years it seems as though the killer didn't kill again. Then, on July 25, 1981, Mary Elizabeth Critchley, a thirty-seven-year-old college student, went missing. Mary Elizabeth, Betsy to her friends, was having dental work done. She traveled to Massachusetts to see a dentist who worked on her teeth at almost no charge so he could get experience. After her appointment, the dentist and his assistant dropped Mary Elizabeth off at the interstate, where she planned to hitchhike on I-95 back to her home in Waterbury, Vermont. This was the last time she was seen alive. Two weeks later her body was found in Unity, New Hampshire. However, it took almost an extra two months before anyone identified her.

At first, Mary Elizabeth was not included in the list of the Connecticut River valley victims, since her killer didn't stab her; in fact, her cause of death was unknown. Since the Connecticut River Valley Killer stabbed his victims, investigators, at first, believed she was linked to another string of rapes and murders.

|||||||||||||||||||||||||||||||||||||||||||||||||||||||||||||||||||||||||||||||||||||||

Gary Schaefer

Mary Elizabeth Critchley was first thought to be a victim of a serial rapist and murderer, Gary Schaefer. Schaefer, a native Vermonter, raped and murdered a thirteen-year-old girl in Springfield in 1979. His victim, Sherry Nastasia, lived with her family in an apartment complex managed by Schaefer's brother. He then went on to rape and murder Theresa Fenton in 1981. Deana Buxton survived his attack in 1982. While being investigated for Deana's rape, Schaefer went on to rape and murder Catherine Richards. There were witnesses to Catherine's abduction, and their descriptions matched Schaefer.

While police were preparing their case against Schaefer, Catherine's mother wrote to Schaefer, accusing him of her daughter's murder. She reminded him of his religious beliefs—Schaefer was a member of the fundamentalist Christadelphian Church—and pressed him to confess. It worked; Schaefer confessed to his crimes. As part of a plea bargain, he pled guilty to kidnapping, sexual assault, and second-degree murder. He was sentenced to thirty years to life at the federal penitentiary in Leavenworth, Kansas.

|||||||||||||||||||||||||||||||||||||||||||||||||||||||||||||||||||||||||||||||||||||||

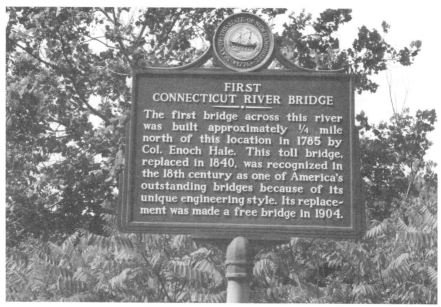

FIRST
CONNECTICUT RIVER BRIDGE
The first bridge across this river
was built approximately ¼ mile
north of this location in 1785 by
Col. Enoch Hale. This toll bridge,
replaced in 1840, was recognized in
the 18th century as one of America's
outstanding bridges because of its
unique engineering style. Its replace-
ment was made a free bridge in 1904.

Sign noting the River Valley Area in Vermont

Almost three years later, on May 30, 1984, sixteen-year-old Bernice Courtemanche was the next to go missing. Bernice lived with her boyfriend's parents, Janet and Arthur Berry. On the thirtieth she had left their home to go visit Teddy, her boyfriend, in Newport, New Hampshire. There were many reported sightings of Bernice, but none were ever verified. Police began a missing-persons case on Bernice immediately because she was underage. She also did not seem to be inclined to run away. She was happy with her boyfriend and seemed to enjoy living at the Berrys' home. She also went missing a few days before payday at the nursing home where she worked. Police believe if she had left willingly, she would have picked up the $113 check before disappearing.

For almost two years, Bernice was on the list of missing persons, until on April 19, 1986. Two men came across skeletal remains about twenty-five yards from a logging track in the northern part of Kellyville, New Hampshire. The remains were partly submerged in a small stream. Much of the skeleton was missing, but investigators found the skull and the upper part of the torso, which was still wrapped in a jacket. There were a few other bones nearby, but the rest had either been washed away in the stream or scavenged by animals. On the twenty-second, the skeleton was identified as Bernice. The medical examiner, Dr. Henry Ryan, was able to determine, despite only having a partial skeleton, that Bernice had been stabbed to death.

During the two years that Bernice was missing, the killer had not been idle. In fact, within two months of Bernice going missing, he had taken another woman. Coworkers reported that Ellen Fried, a twenty-seven-year-old nurse, went missing. She had missed her Friday and Saturday shifts at Valley Regional Hospital in Claremont, New Hampshire. Also on that Friday night, a patrol officer found an old Chevelle parked on Jarvis Lane, a dirt road in a wooded area only a couple of miles from Clermont City Center. The car was locked and nothing seemed to be out of place. When the car was still there the next day, an officer went to check on the owner. However, Ellen had moved earlier in the year, and her information hadn't been updated. On Sunday, the police organized a thorough search of the area around where they'd found Ellen's car. On Monday the search intensified, with a local pilot searching from the air, ATVs riding through the woods, and bloodhounds trying to find her. The last confirmed contact with Ellen was when she called her sister from a pay phone at Leo's Market, a convenience store on Main Street in Claremont, shortly after leaving work on Thursday night. She worked the three-to-eleven shift at the hospital, and her sister lived in California, so it was three hours earlier there. The phone call seemed normal . . . mostly. At one point during the call, she mentioned a car driving through the parking lot. It spooked Ellen enough that she went and started her car before she ended the call with her sister. Perhaps that car had been someone watching her. Someone stalking her. All her sister knew was that there had been something about it that had unsettled Ellen.

Police found no leads, and Ellen became the second missing woman from Claremont in less than two months. Missing until September 19, 1985, when two men had gone into the woods to do some target shooting, and they found human remains. The men found her about fifty feet from the abandoned railway tracks that were being used as a jogging path that ran along the Sugar River. All that was left of her remains were a few bones and a single sandal. It took twelve days after they found the bones to confirm that it was Ellen Fried. The identification was even harder because no one knew what clothes Ellen had been wearing the night she had gone missing. Had she been wearing her nurse's whites, or had she changed into street clothes? No one knew. The spot where they found Ellen's remains was only three miles away from where Bernice Courtemanche's body would be found about six months later.

Eva Morse left home on July 10, 1985, to hitchhike to work. She arrived at work at 7:00 a.m. but left before punching her time card. She told her boss she was sick and needed to go home. She never made it home. At first, not much was done to locate Eva. Many believed that because of her troubled past, she may have taken off, leaving her daughter behind. Not her family, though. Eva's sister, Noreen, returned to the area from Maine and started putting up ads and flyers. Noreen knew that Eva would never abandon her daughter, Jenny. Once Noreen began to draw attention to Eva's disappearance, the investigation picked up. However, police were dealing with a serious lack of manpower, and there was nothing they had to use to trace Eva's presence, because she didn't have a car. Shortly after the local

The grave of Eva Morse. She was last seen hitchhiking on July 10, 1986.

paper ran an article on Eva, a woman came forward to say that on July 10, she had picked up a woman matching Eva's description. According to this woman, her passenger seemed to be going to Claremont, but the driver was only going as far as the Charlestown-Claremont town line. So she dropped her passenger off at the veterinary clinic where she worked in Knight's Hill. Eva, if that was her, was last seen trying to hitch a ride north toward Claremont. Within five minutes she was gone, but no one saw her catch a ride.

On April 25, 1986, two brothers found her remains about 500 feet from where Mary Elizabeth Critchley had been found. Even stranger, these two men had been part of the group who found Mary Elizabeth's remains five years before. Identification did not take long in this case, since the police were quite sure whose bones had been found in Unity's woods. They sent the dental materials to Eva's dentist, and he was able to ID her within a few hours.

Only eleven days before searchers found Eva Morse's remains, another woman was murdered. Thirty-six-year-old Lynda Moore had been taking advantage of one of the first warm days of the year to do some yard work and sun herself by the pool. Her home in Saxtons River, Vermont, was a beautiful old house that the Moores had been fixing up. It was also located on a bend in the road that forced people to slow down. Meaning everyone who traveled the road got a good look at their home. Also, it was well known that Lynda enjoyed sunbathing by the pool in her bikini. Some men might be more inclined to pay attention to what was happening in that yard that had such an appealing view.

The grave of Lynda Moore, murdered in her home on April 15, 1986

Unfortunately for Lynda, no one saw what happened to her that warm April afternoon. All we know is that Lynda was alive at 12:45 p.m. when she spoke to her husband, Steve, on the phone. However, when he called her later around 1:00 p.m., the line was busy. At 3:00 p.m., Steve headed home, with one of his employees following him in another vehicle. When Steve got to his house he found Lynda's shoes still sitting next to a lawn chair near their back door. He found her lying on the kitchen floor in a pool of blood. He called an ambulance, then called his employee, who had stayed in the driveway, for help. He even used the phone to call a friend and his parents to let them know what had happened. When the ambulance driver got there, he knew Lynda was long past help, and he asked if Steve had called the police. Steve was behaving disconnected and odd, and the police suspected that Steve had killed her. They soon realized that he had a solid alibi for the day and could not have killed his wife. There was no shortage of sightings of strange men seen in the area, but none of these leads panned out.

John Philipin, a psychologist who worked with the police on these cases, suggested this scenario for what happened that day: Philipin believes that the killer watched Lynda for a time as she sunned herself in the yard. At 12:45 p.m., he saw her hurry into the house to answer the call from her husband. She left her sandals behind in her rush to get to the phone. The killer would have followed her into the house, and once he heard the phone call end, he approached her. Lynda was an assertive woman and would have demanded he leave her home. He'd attacked her with his knife. She tried to defend herself, but he was stronger than she was, and armed. The attack was brutal; the killer stabbed Lynda more than twenty-four times. He then left the scene, undetected by any living human.

Of course, this is all conjecture, but what we do know is that the attack happened in her kitchen, and she did try to fight off her assailant. Philipin also came to believe that the killer had meant to take Lynda from her home. However, she had put up too fierce of a fight, and he had been forced to kill her in the house. This would account for most of the differences from the other murders.

Barbara Agnew was a thirty-eight-year-old divorced mother living in Norwich, Vermont, and was working as a nurse and going to school to get a bachelor's degree in nursing. She shared custody of her son, Neal, with her ex-husband, and he alternated one week with her, then one week with his father. On the weekend of January 10, 1987, Barbara drove to Stratton to meet with a man she had met while traveling the previous year. They spent the day skiing and had dinner at a local restaurant. Barbara's friend offered to let her stay with him and his daughters at his condo, but Barbara decided to head home despite the snow that was falling. She was never seen again.

Her friends back in Norwich didn't worry when she wasn't home that Sunday. Her son was staying with his father that week, and she didn't start classes until that Thursday. However, as the days passed without a word from her, they began to worry.

While all this was going on, another mystery was unfolding in Hartford, Vermont. On Sunday, January 11, the plow truck drivers were forced to plow around a vehicle that appeared to be stuck near the back of the building at a rest area on I-91. It was partly on the lawn, with its nose sticking out into the access lane, and the driver's-side door was left open. Plow drivers assumed that the car was stuck in the snow, and the driver had left the vehicle. They expected the driver would be back with a tow truck to haul the car away. By the end of the day on Sunday, the plow drivers reported the abandoned vehicle to the rest area attendant, and the next day the state police arranged for someone to tow the car to a Sunoco station in White River Junction.

Then, on Tuesday morning at another rest area south of White River Junction, a young attendant noticed a man reaching into one of the dumpsters and pulling out a garment. As the attendant approached the dumpsters, the other man dropped the clothes and walked away. In the container, the young man found a ski jacket, a sweater, and a sweatshirt, all in very good condition. He found a wallet in the ski jacket. There was no money in the wallet, but there was an ID card from Mary Hitchcock Memorial Hospital in Hanover, New Hampshire. Listed on the card was Barbara Agnew's name, address, and phone number, which he tried calling. When he couldn't reach anyone, he turned the clothes and wallet over to a clerk for the highway department. She tried to call the hospital listed on Barbara's ID and was rebuffed by an ill-tempered receptionist. The next day the clerk tried again and reached a more sympathetic response. This receptionist called Barbara's emergency contact, her ex-husband, Dr. Douglas Talon. Dr. Talon contacted one of his ex-wife's best friends, and they went to check on her apartment. When they found it empty and unchanged since Barbara had left on Saturday, they called the Norwich Police Department. This was on Wednesday morning, and Barbara was now officially a missing person.

Officer Jim Cushing headed to the rest area where Barbara's clothes had been discovered, and he spoke to the attendant who had found them. There was nothing else amiss according to the attendant, other than the abandoned vehicle that was now sitting in White River Junction. Cushing checked the plates on the car, and sure enough, it was registered to Barbara Agnew. Cushing and Sergeant Ted LeClair of the state police went to investigate Barbara's car. They found it with the door still ajar and blood spotted and smeared on the interior.

By the next morning, Thursday, January 15, state police had gathered to search for Barbara. Police and firefighters from Hartford also joined in the search for her and any clues. They sifted through the snow, where they found some hair and blood stains. The mobile crime lab arrived, and they found more blood and hair and some fibers. The evidence seemed to form a diagonal path through the parking area, from where Barbara's car had been to a spot across the lot.

Police interviewed both her current boyfriend and the friend she had spent the day with. Neither seemed a likely suspect, but there was something else that was strange. Barbara's ski clothes had been taken from her car after it had been abandoned. The plow drivers had first seen her car between 11:00 p.m. Saturday and 1:00 a.m. Sunday. At that time they had briefly checked the car, and they believed that those items went missing after they had driven by that first time. Had someone stolen those items later on, or had Barbara's attacker come back to her car? The area had a shady reputation as a hookup spot, and several assaults had been reported at this rest area. So it could have been someone checking the area out who took advantage of the open car sitting in the lot.

Police were also trying to figure out why Barbara had stopped at this rest area when she was only ten minutes away from her home. A woman called in with a potential answer. She had been traveling on I-91 that Saturday night and had seen a hand-lettered sign propped up by the rest stop, advertising a coffee break. Knowing that local organizations sometimes sold coffee and snacks during bad weather to raise money, the caller had pulled into the rest area, but she was ill at ease. The area seemed deserted, where there should be activity. She decided not to stop and drove through. Perhaps Barbara had stopped in for a quick snack, and it cost her her life.

No one could be sure about what happened in that rest area, other than that a violent confrontation had taken place. There was little hope of finding Barbara Agnew alive, and on March 28 everyone's fears were confirmed.

Despite there still being a foot of snow on the ground, a woman from Hartland, Vermont, took some visiting friends on a hike in the woods. In a small clearing about a half mile from her home, they found Barbara's body, facedown in the snow. After Barbara's body was found, a plow truck driver came forward. That Sunday morning he had been plowing the Advent Hill area, where they'd found

Barbara's body, and he had seen car tracks in the snow. The tracks were noticeable because the storm was so bad that no one was out driving that morning. Also according to the tracks, the car had first pulled into one family's driveway on the road, then pulled back out onto the road; it then stopped again at another family's home, where it appeared the vehicle turned around and headed back down Advent Hill, the way it had come. The plow driver knew that both houses belonged to families who lived in the area only in the summertime. So he knew it wasn't anyone from either family. Unfortunately, the plow driver didn't notice if there were any footprints in the snow, because of limited visibility, and he needed to focus on his own vehicle maneuvering up the treacherous (at least on this morning) road. He did think that the tracks looked recent, but he had difficulty remembering what time he'd driven through the area.

This time the body had only been in the woods for a few winter months, and the cold had preserved it. At the rest area, she had fought her attacker. The killer had left the car door open because it had been damaged when he attacked Barbara. During the attack in the parking lot, she had either made it back to her car or never left it and threw her car into reverse. However, she hadn't been able to shut the driver's-side door, and the force of backing into the snow with it open damaged the door, preventing it from being closed again. She was then forced, at knife point, to the killer's vehicle. He then drove her to a predetermined spot (he passed several potential dump sites on the way to Advent Hill), where he forced her into the woods. There were signs that she had fought desperately for her life, but he had forced her to her knees and stabbed her in the neck from behind. His first blow severed the jugular, and she would have been almost immediately unconscious. The killer then went on to inflict multiple stab wounds. He continued to stab even after she died. This was the first time that investigators had been able to dissect the crime scene when the killer was able to act out his fantasy without interruption.

On the night of August 6, 1988, Jane Boroski became the last known victim of the Connecticut River Valley Killer. Only Jane was luckier than the other women who had crossed paths with him. She lived to tell what happened to her.

That morning, Jane had fought with her boyfriend, Dennis. Their relationship had gotten rocky since she had found out she was pregnant. So after spending her day upset and a bit angry, Jane decided to go to the Cheshire County Fair on her own. While there, she had fun and spent most of her time with Dennis's mother, whom she met with on the Midway. They played games and managed to win seven stuffed animals for the baby. Jane lined the animals up in the backseat of her car and headed home a little after midnight. She decided to stop at the Country Store on her way home and buy a soda from one of the vending machines. She sat back down in her car, and, as she was opening a can of soda, another vehicle pulled up next to her. The other driver got out of his vehicle, a Jeep Wagoneer or something similar; he stepped up to her door and asked if the pay phone was working. As she answered that she didn't know, he opened her car door and grabbed her wrist. He demanded she go with him. She tried to pull away from him, but his grip was too strong. She pleaded with him not to hurt her because she was pregnant, but

Store parking lot where Jane Boroski stopped on August 6, 1988

it did not seem to faze him. Convinced that she and her baby were in danger, Jane lashed out, kicking at him, desperate to get away. She even kicked out the windshield of her car in her desperation. Her attacker then pulled a knife out and dragged her out of the car. He dropped the knife as he was pulling her from the car, and Jane tried to run but he grabbed her. He was determined to get her into his vehicle, but Jane pushed him away. She tried to run to the traffic she could see on Route 10, beyond the parking lot, but she barely made it a few feet before he grabbed her and threw her to the ground. She did her best to shield her baby but he stabbed her over and over. Then, he was gone. She saw him drive off and for the first time got a good look at his face.

Jane struggled to her feet and dragged herself to her car. She was having a hard time breathing and was bleeding from her neck and chest. She got into the car and managed to start it despite severe damage to her hand. Jane, she had to get help fast. She pulled back onto the road and started looking for a house with their lights on, but Jane soon realized that she had caught up to her attacker's vehicle. She was terrified, convinced that he knew it was her, and she thought he would try to run her off the road. She pulled into the driveway of a friend. There were no lights on, but she tried rousing people by blaring her car's horn. When this didn't work, she managed to get out of her car and get to the door just as her friend was opening it. She begged him to call an ambulance for her. During this time her friend heard a vehicle stop at the end of his driveway, and it looked like a Jeep Wagoneer. Jane was sure her attacker had come back to kill her, but the vehicle moved on after a moment.

The police and ambulance came, and Jane was rushed into surgery. She had been stabbed twenty-three to twenty-seven times, her jugular had been cut, both lungs had collapsed, the tendons in her knee and thumb had been severed, and she lost part of her liver. However, her baby had, miraculously, not been harmed in the attack. Jane would make a physical recovery, but she has not recovered mentally. She suffers from depression, has had nervous breakdowns, and has developed several compulsive disorders. Her daughter was born two weeks early, and there were complications. Little Jessica Lyn spent eight days in the hospital, and according to Jane, her daughter has mild cerebral palsy.

Once Jane was well enough to speak with police, she was able to give a description of her attacker. He had a thin face with close-set eyes, a high forehead, and dark-blonde hair that was combed straight back.

In October 1997, Gary Westover made a confession to his uncle, Howard Minnon, a retired sheriff's deputy from New Hampshire. Westover, a paraplegic, told his uncle about one night when three of his friends had come by his home. They forced him to accompany them as they abducted a woman, then killed her, and dumped her body in the woods. Gary gave his uncle the names of the men and expressed his grief and shame over what happened.

According to the family, they contacted law enforcement but were not believed. Minnon vowed to never speak to the police again. Westover died in 1998, and Howard died in 2006. Another member of the family sent a letter to Barbara Agnew's sister, Anna. Anna then forwarded the letter to private investigator Lynn-Marie Carty, who was investigating another man many believe to be the Connecticut River Valley Killer, Michael Nicholaou.

Both Carty and Philipin believed Westover's story and thought it did conform to what could have happened to Barbara. There would also be little reason for Westover to make up a story like this. Unfortunately, the names that Gary shared with his uncle are lost. There may be a record in some law enforcement file, but no one who knows those names is alive now, although, when pressed, one of Gary's aunts did say that the name Nicholaou sounded familiar.

Michael Nicholaou was a decorated Vietnam veteran until he was charged with murder and attempted murder for shooting at civilians. The army dropped the charges, but Nicholaou was bitter. He sued the army over the incident after leaving the service in disgrace.

After the war, Nicholaou married Michelle Ashley, and they had two children together. They lived in Holyoke, Massachusetts, but spent a lot of time visiting Michelle's family in the Connecticut River valley. However, their relationship was rocky. Michelle told her family that she was planning on leaving Nicholaou after her sister's wedding in November 1988. She told her mother that Nicholaou was controlling, unstable, and most likely suffering from posttraumatic stress disorder. Her mother stopped to visit in December 1988 and found their home abandoned. There were Christmas gifts still under the tree, and the fridge was full of rotting food. From this time on, Nicholaou moved around a lot. He stayed with his mother in Virginia, friends in Florida, and old army buddies all across the country. No one has heard anything from Michelle since that time. When Michelle's mother hired Carty, it didn't take her long to track down Nicholaou. At first, he denied even knowing Michelle but then told Carty that Michelle had run off with a drug dealer, and he didn't know where she was. At that time Nicholaou was living in Georgia.

Nicholaou's second wife, Aileen Nicholaou, left him after he broke her shoulder. Aileen moved in with her sister in Tampa, Florida, with her twenty-year-old daughter, Terrin Bowman. Nicholaou tracked them down and, on December 31, 2005, killed both women and himself during a standoff with police.

Lynn-Marie Carty is convinced that Michael Nicholaou is the Connecticut River Valley Killer, and Jane Boroski thought Nicholaou looked similar to her attacker. There is a problem though: at the time of the first three murders, Nicholaou was still living in Virginia. He was even involved in a high-profile obscenity case over the porn store he had been running. There is also no physical evidence linking him to any of the murders. So, it is unlikely that Nicholaou is responsible for these crimes.

At this time there have been no arrests and no known victims since the attack on Jane Boroski. If you have any information about this case, please contact Captain J. P. Sinclair of the Vermont Major Crimes Unit, or anonymously at https://vsp.vermont.gov/tipsubmit, or contact coldcaseunit@dos.nh.gov for the New Hampshire Cold Case Unit.

Rhode Island

CAMILLA "CAM" LYMAN'S MURDER

Hopkinton

....

SOMETIMES I WORRY THAT I'LL NEVER
BE TRULY COMFORTABLE IN MY BODY,
THAT I'LL NEVER OBTAIN PEACE.

—ANONYMOUS

The Lyman family plot in the Westwood Cemetery

Camilla Lyman was born in the affluent Boston suburb of Westwood on September 4, 1932. She grew up with a busy father and emotionally distant mother. Her joy in life was dogs. Camilla was a professional breeder and handler of purebred, champion dogs. She usually worked with Clumber spaniels, a long-coated English breed of hunting dog.

In November 1968, when Camilla was thirty-six years old, her father, Arthur Lyman, died, and after his death, Camilla began wearing men's clothes and going by the more masculine name of Cam (Camilla legally changed "his" name in 1985). It is speculated that Cam may have been taking steroids prescribed for his dogs, since his hair started thinning and he was able to grow a thin mustache. Cam was also known to be volatile, often having angry outbursts if his dogs lost.

Cam's gravestone

He also began to have less contact with his family, and in 1984 he sold the family home in Westwood and bought a forty-acre estate in Hopkinton, Rhode Island. He hired George O'Neil, a friend and fellow dog breeder he had known since 1981, to work as the caretaker on the estate. George took care of the house and ran errands for Cam. He was even picking up packages and cashing checks for him. This left Cam with more time to care for his fifty-eight dogs.

Most people considered Lyman a rich eccentric, living as a man and rarely leaving his estate unless it was for a dog show. It was even rumored that Cam kept a briefcase filled with jewels with him at all times, even when he was sleeping. Everyone agreed he was devoted to his dogs, so it was a surprise to people when one day Cam was just gone.

George O'Neil claimed that he and Cam had argued about the dogs over the phone one evening in July, and then the call suddenly ended. When he went to the estate the next day, the phone had been ripped from the wall, and Cam was not at home. According to O'Neil, the case of jewels and some of Cam's clothing were gone as well. O'Neil did not report Lyman missing, claiming he assumed that Cam had gone to the United Kingdom in order to get a sex change. O'Neil said that Cam had frequently spoken about getting it done, and he had assumed that is where Cam went. O'Neil also maintained that the reclusive Lyman would often go away for months at a time, so he wasn't concerned that he hadn't heard from his friend.

For a year, no report was made to the police regarding Cam going missing. The family started to become concerned when they found out that Cam had not sent out Christmas cards, as was his custom. His sister wrote to him, and when she didn't receive a response the family notified police in December 1988. There was no formal investigation of the disappearance because O'Neil informed them that Cam had gone to the United Kingdom to get a sex change. In the meantime, O'Neil had taken control of Cam's dogs, and he showed them as his own. He was also taking advantage of his power of attorney to cash checks from Cam's accounts.

In August 1988, Cam Lyman's family hired Charles Allen, a private investigator. He looked for Cam in the United States and was unable to find any trace of him. When he went to the estate to search the house for any clues as to what had happened, O'Neil refused to let him on the grounds, as was his right as power of attorney. Allen then made inquiries with his contacts in the UK transgender scene to look for anyone who fit Cam's description, but no one had seen him. In 1995, when nothing could be found about Cam, his family had him declared legally dead by the probate court. The family settled with George O'Neil, letting him keep the estate in Hopkinton while the family retained Cam's $2 million trust.

On September 24, 1997, Hopkinton's new police chief, John Scunico, decided to look into the missing-person case. He brought cadaver-sniffing dogs to the estate, which O'Neil had sold to a couple who also bred dogs. During the search of the property, one of the owners noticed a foul smell coming from the septic tank. When he removed the cover he saw a skull floating in the muck. The medical examiner identified the remains as Camilla "Cam" Lyman. Cam had been shot and then dropped in the septic tank, with a cinder block tied to his body.

Cam was laid to rest in October 1998. Unfortunately, due to legal reasons, Cam's ashes could not be dropped on Madison Square Garden during the Westminster Dog Show, as he had requested. Instead, he was buried in the family plot in Westwood, Massachusetts. It is believed that Cam died on July 20, 1987. It has now been thirty years since Cam was lost, and the case remains unsolved.

Theory

There is only one likely suspect in the case, but there is no evidence to prove that George O'Neil had anything to do with the death of Cam Lyman. It is possible that he did, in good faith, believe that Cam had left the country and didn't tell anyone where he was going or what he was doing. Perhaps O'Neil took advantage of the opportunity provided by his friend's absence, then the longer that Cam was gone, the harder it was for O'Neil to notify police about the situation. It is also possible that O'Neil knows what happened to Lyman, but kept quiet about his friend's end from either fear or greed. It could also be possible that a person (or people) knew about Cam's case of jewels, broke into the home, and killed Cam for the jewels. It was hardly a secret that Cam had money, and someone could have targeted him. We may never know the answers.

If you have any information about the murder of Cam Lyman, please contact the Hopkinton Police Department in Hopkinton, Rhode Island, at (401) 377-7750.

SUNNY VON BÜLOW'S ATTEMPTED MURDER OR UNFORTUNATE ACCIDENT

Newport

....

THIS WAS A TRAGEDY AND IT SATISFIED ALL
OF ARISTOTLE'S DEFINITIONS OF TRAGEDY. EVERYONE IS
WOUNDED, SOME FATALLY.

—CLAUS VON BÜLOW

Here is a case that seems impossible to understand and be impartial about. If you are not a member of this very niche society, you probably won't understand the acceptable social norms and, therefore, can't determine the proper behavior of the people involved. If you *are* a member of that group, you likely know the people involved and are more likely to let your friendship/loyalty bias your viewpoint. They say that it is easier for the rich to get away with murder in the United States, but when the rich are the victims it is also difficult to investigate the crime.

On December 22, 1980, the emergency room of Newport Hospital was, again, treating Martha "Sunny" von Bülow. For the second time in less than a year, Sunny had slipped into a coma and was being rushed to the hospital for

The gates of Clarendon Court, Newport, Rhode Island

care. On December 26, 1979, Sunny had been taken to Newport Hospital in a coma. She recovered and was diagnosed as hypoglycemic. Now, just five days short of a year, she was back in the hospital under similar conditions, only this time Sunny did not recover. The question is, How did all this come to be?

Martha "Sunny" Crawford was born into privilege. At the age of four, she inherited $100 million from her father, who had been the chairman of Columbia Gas and Electric Company, and her mother was an heiress coming from the family that founded the International Shoe Company. Despite her wealth, Sunny was not happy; she was frequently depressed and often thought about death—leading some to argue that Sunny had attempted suicide and had been prevented from completing the act. Sunny married Prince Alfie von Auersperg in July 1957, becoming Princess von Auersperg. The couple seemed to be truly in love, but incompatible. Despite their love and having two children, Annie-Laurie ("Ala") and Alexander, the couple ended up divorcing in 1965. Alfie and Sunny did remain on friendly terms after their marriage.

||||||||||||||||||||||||||||||||||||||||||||||||||||||||||||||||||||||||||||||||||||

On an odd note, Sunny's first husband was in a car accident, in 1983, that left him in an irreversible coma until his death in 1992. One can only imagine the heartbreak of Ala and Alexander having not one but both of their parents lingering in comas for such extended periods of time.

||||||||||||||||||||||||||||||||||||||||||||||||||||||||||||||||||||||||||||||||||||

While separated, Sunny met a charming young man, Claus von Bülow. Claus Borberg was born on August 11, 1926, in Copenhagen, Denmark. His parents divorced when he was four years old, and after World War II, Claus changed his name to his mother's familial name, since his father was known as a Nazi sympathizer, and Claus wished to distance himself from his father's reputation. Claus graduated from Trinity College in Cambridge, England, and worked as a barrister. When he met Sunny von Auersperg, Claus was working for J. P. Getty as his personal assistant. He stopped working for Getty two years after he married Sunny, allegedly because she wanted him to be spending his time with her.

The couple appeared happy, at least to outsiders, and on April 15, 1967, they had their only child together, Cosima von Bülow. The birth was reportedly difficult for Sunny, and afterward she had no interest in a sexual relationship with her husband. She gave Claus permission to discreetly seek companionship outside their marriage. They managed to keep up the appearance of a happy family until December 26, 1979, when Sunny slipped into her first coma.

Up until this incident, Claus reportedly had a close relationship with his stepchildren, but after the first coma, they became suspicious of their stepfather. Maria Schrallhammer, who had been Sunny's maid since right after she married for the first time, was concerned about Claus's behavior on the day that Sunny was ill. According to Maria, Sunny had been in obvious distress, and when she suggested they call a doctor, Claus rebuffed her. It wasn't until eight hours had passed and Sunny's son, Alexander, intervened that Claus agreed to get Sunny to the hospital. Sunny recovered but was diagnosed as being hypoglycemic.

However, Maria was now skeptical of her mistress's husband; she suspected foul play. Several weeks later, Maria was cleaning the bedroom closets at Clarendon Court, the name of the von Bülows' Newport Mansion, when she saw a black bag that belonged to Claus. She unzipped the bag and checked out its contents. "I really didn't know why I did it," she would later testify. "It just . . . happened." In the bag, she found some pills, a vial of a paste-like substance, and a powder. She took this to Ala, who brought it to the family physician to identify the contents. The pills and paste were both Valium, and the powder was secobarbital, a powerful barbiturate. Although the form of the pills was unusual, it wasn't anything that hadn't been prescribed for the couple in the past. So there was nothing Ala, Alexander, or Maria could do other than keep an eye on Claus and Sunny.

In April 1980, Sunny had another, smaller episode. She was taken to a New York hospital for tests. The tests reaffirmed the diagnosis of hypoglycemia, and Sunny was told she needed to be on a strict diet. No sugars and no alcohol. Sunny followed the advice and seemed to be doing very well. She maintained her diet and attended her daughter's wedding to Franz Kneissl. However, Maria was remaining vigilant, and at Thanksgiving that year she found a new addition to the black bag, a vial of insulin and syringes. Maria told Alexander but said nothing to Sunny. After Thanksgiving, Sunny was again ill; this time she had overdosed herself with aspirin while suffering from a sinus infection. It was Claus who notified Maria of Sunny's illness and called 911. This time, Sunny spent six days in the hospital; she had taken sixty aspirin, enough to kill herself.

Then, right before Christmas, the von Bülows went to Clarendon Court for a few days for a break from preholiday stress. They would need to return to New York City for Christmas to be with Sunny's mother, who was too ill to travel to Rhode Island. Claus suggested that Maria stay in New York, since the trip would be for a short time, but before they left, Maria checked Claus's bags and saw the black bag and its contents in his luggage. She would never see Sunny awake again.

On the evening of December 21, things seemed normal for the family. At dinner, there was a disagreement on whether Sunny ate the main course, but all agreed that she insisted on having a large ice cream sundae with caramel sauce. Then everyone went to see a movie at the local cinema. After the movie, Alexander, Cosima, and Sunny gathered in the library while Claus went to his study to do some work. Sunny left to go to her private bathroom for a while but returned with a drink. Alexander thought it was ginger ale. Claus came through the library, asking if anyone wanted anything from the kitchen. Sunny asked him to bring her some of the chicken soup from dinner. Before Claus returned from the kitchen, Alexander noticed his mother was becoming weak and lethargic. Alexander had to carry his mother to bed. He then headed to the kitchen to get Claus, who was still getting Sunny's soup ready. Claus was on a long-distance call, so Alexander went up to check on his mother. He found her crawling back to her bed after going to the bathroom. Claus then came up to the bedroom, and he and Alexander got Sunny back into bed. Alexander then left for the night to meet up with some friends for a holiday party.

The next morning, when Sunny hadn't gotten up by 11:00 a.m., Claus went to check on her. He found her unconscious on the floor in her bathroom, with her head under the toilet bowl. She had a cut on her lip, her nightgown was bunched around her waist, and she lay in a puddle of urine. Claus got Alexander, and they checked on Sunny. She was still alive, but ice cold. She was taken to Newport Hospital, where she went into cardiac arrest. The doctors managed to resuscitate her, but they knew her condition was more serious than they could deal with effectively. They transferred Sunny to a Boston hospital, but her coma was determined to be irreversible.

Claus's stepchildren immediately suspected him of foul play but did not want the publicity that a police investigation would bring, since their mother was a private person. Ala and Alexander hired a private investigator, and, with Maria's guidance on what to look for, they headed to Clarendon Court. They were looking for the black bag Maria had seen with drugs and syringes. They claimed to have found the bag and its contents in the closet of Claus and Sunny's bedroom. The needles were sent to a private lab in Long Island for testing. Reports came back that the needles were encrusted with insulin. At this time the family contacted the police. The police searched the home and interviewed Claus.

In July 1981, a grand jury indicted Claus for two attempts on Sunny's life, and he was arraigned later that month. The proceedings were already a media circus. The case had all the sensational aspects people love: the rich involved in murder plots, affairs, and drug use. Better than any daytime soap opera, and this case even had a soap opera star involved.

In February 1982, the trial started; jurors heard from a variety of medical experts, and both Alexander von Auersperg and Maria Schrallhammer were star witnesses against Claus. Alexandra Isles, who was a famous soap opera star, heiress, and Claus's lover, testified that she had given several ultimatums to Claus about leaving Sunny—thus providing the prosecution a second motive for Claus wanting to murder his wife. The first motive was money. Banker Morris Gurley testified that Claus would get approximately $14 million if Sunny died.

The defense called witnesses to attest to Sunny's previous attempts at suicide and her drug use, but they failed to convince the jury. On March 16, 1982, the jury found Claus von Bülow guilty of two counts of attempted murder. He was later sentenced to ten years for the first attempt and twenty years for the second. Claus remained free with a $1 million bail pending his appeal.

For his appeal, Claus hired Alan Dershowitz, a lawyer and Harvard law professor. The case for retrial involved the illegal search and seizure of the black bag, the inconsistencies of testimonies, and the failure of the prosecution to share interview notes of witnesses with the defense. Dershowitz won the appeal, and a second trial of Claus was scheduled.

The second trial began in April 1985, and the prosecution's case was much the same, only that no information about the black bag or its contents could be mentioned. This time the defense was also more aggressive in its cross-examination of the witnesses. Sunny's maid, Maria, was found to have not mentioned that insulin was in the black bag in her original interview and remembered it only after the insulin had been found and tested. This was in contrast to her testimony in the first trial. Defense attorney Thomas Puccio also got Maria to admit that she had previously lied under oath to protect Sunny. Puccio also questioned Alexander about plans he and the family had made to try to pay off Claus if he would renounce his inheritance from Sunny. This helped call into question Alexander's testimony. It appeared as if he were more interested in the money, thus giving him a motive to make his stepfather look guilty. The medical testimony suffered from the lack of the black bag, and the medical expert admitted that there was a 10 percent chance that Sunny's coma was not caused by an injection of insulin.

Alexandra Isles was dramatically forced to testify; she had fled to Europe to avoid the trial and was escorted by police into the courtroom. In this trial, she testified that Claus had told her that he had seen Sunny take a sleeping pill, drink a lot of alcoholic eggnog, and then take a Seconal, a sedative. He watched her lie unconscious for hours, but he could not go through with watching her die so he called for help.

The arguments ended on June 5, 1981, and on June 10, the jury came back with a not-guilty verdict. Claus was free to go, but he still had much to deal with after his acquittal. His daughter, Cosima, had been disinherited by her maternal grandmother, and Ala and Alexander were suing him for $56 million. Claus dropped the claim to Sunny's estate in return for Cosima being reinstated in her grandmother's will. His stepchildren dropped the lawsuit against him, since all they wanted was for him not to get Sunny's money.

Did Claus try to kill Sunny, or did he fail to act when his wife was in distress? Was the case only a ploy by Sunny's family to keep her money? If the family had gone to the police with their suspicions instead of to a private investigator, would the case against Claus have been made? Unfortunately, we will likely never know. All we do know is that Claus von Bülow lives under a cloud of suspicion, and Sunny's three children were deprived of their mother. There was also a rift between the siblings because Cosima stood by her father during the whole affair. As for Sunny, she lived on in a vegetative state for twenty-eight years until she passed away on December 6, 2008, and Claus, as of late 2018, is still alive and active in the social scene.

Alan Dershowitz wrote the book *Reversal of Fortune: Inside the von Bülow Case*, which recounts the story of the von Bülow trial. He has also gone on to work on other famous cases such as O. J. Simpson's murder trial.

THE MURDER OF RITA BOUCHARD

Pawtucket/Providence

....

DEATH IS AN ABSOLUTE MYSTERY. WE ARE ALL VULNERABLE
TO IT; IT'S WHAT MAKES LIFE INTERESTING AND SUSPENSEFUL.

—JEANNE MOREAU

O n February 1, 1947, Joseph Curry was going for a walk along Pawtucket's Ten Mile River when he saw something strange on the side of his path. To his horror, he realized it was the body of a young woman. Her throat had been slit and she had been stabbed about thirty times. Her killer had laid her body out on her gray coat in the muddy ground about one hundred feet from the river. A nearby tree bore fresh cut marks, a possible sign left by the killer.

The young woman was Rita Bouchard, a seventeen-year-old worker at the Rhode Island Fabrics Company. Rita and her siblings were wards of the state who lived with their aunt and uncle in North Providence. The family had assumed that Rita, who usually worked the three-to-eleven shift, had spent the night at a friend's house, and they hadn't realized anything had

The tree in the clearing where Rita's body was found

91

Ten-mile path

Clearing where Rita's body was found

happened until they heard the description of a murder victim on the radio that Saturday afternoon.

The coroner examined Rita's body. He found that her throat had been slit so deeply, she was almost decapitated, and the killer had stabbed her mostly in the chest, neck, and back area. Investigators noticed that while her killer had stabbed her thirteen times in the back, her coat only had three holes in it, from what they thought was a stiletto knife. So either her assailant stabbed her, then took her coat off, and then continued to stab her after the garment had been removed, or she had somehow twisted in a way that she was stabbed under her coat. The time of death was set at some time after 6:00 a.m. on Saturday. It was also confirmed that she had not been sexually assaulted.

Because the chief of police was away on vacation, the chief inspector was put in charge of the case, and he assigned most of the detective division to retrace Rita's steps in the hours before her death.

Rita was supposed to be working the three-to-eleven shift on Friday, January 31, but she left work at 5:00 p.m., saying she was feeling unwell. She told her foreman that she was going to see a doctor, then visit with her mother, who was a tuberculosis patient at the state tuberculosis hospital at Wallum Lake, over thirty miles away. She did neither of these things, nor did she return to her aunt and uncle's home.

That evening there were two possible sightings of Rita by bus drivers. The first driver picked up a woman who matched Rita's description and dropped her off near the Main Street Bridge at 5:40 p.m. The second driver knew Rita, and he saw

The Ten Mile River in Pawtucket, Rhode Island

her getting into a car in the downtown area at around 6:00 p.m. Then there was nothing. The police interviewed family, friends, and coworkers, but they had scant information to give police. The closest they had to a lead was that Rita had told her aunt that she was afraid of a man that she had been dating. Rita had often told her aunt she would die a violent death. The police followed this up by checking into her former boyfriends, but they hit a dead end.

For over two weeks, police got nowhere in their investigation. Then a young boy playing near the corner of Armistice Boulevard and Parkside Avenue found an eight-and-a-quarter-inch red-stained knife in the grass. He gave the knife to police, and they matched the knife to the holes left in Rita's coat. The police tried to trace where the knife had come from, but this was another lead that went nowhere.

Then, in the middle of March, one of Rita's close friends, Eugene Pattenaude, was charged with carnal knowledge of an eight-year-old boy. The police knew he was close to Rita, so they pulled him in for interrogation on her murder. Police questioned him for over seventy-two hours before he broke.

Pattenaude told police he had gone to the Rhode Island Fabric Company Friday afternoon to speak with a foreman about returning to work after his leave of absence. Eugene then went downtown and hung out at the Capital Theater until he ran into Rita at around 7:00 p.m. They ended up leaving the theater together and walking down Main Street. They sat on one of the benches until, after a few minutes, a car pulled up. It was a man that Rita knew. All three of them got into the car and drove to Slater Park, but Eugene wanted to go back downtown. So they

The area near where the murder weapon was found

dropped him off in front of the Capital Theater, and as he got out of the car he heard them deciding to go back to the park.

Eugene told police that he started to worry about Rita, so he took the trolley to the park to be sure she was okay. When he got there he found Rita sitting on a bench near the entrance, and she was crying. When he asked her what was wrong, she slapped his face. He repeated the question, and this time she slapped his face and kicked him in the groin, twice. This is when, according to Eugene, his mind went blank. The next thing he remembers is waking up on the ground next to Rita, and there was a knife near her. When he couldn't get a response from her, he got up and walked out of the park, then took a bus home. He got home at around 10:00 p.m. that night. He claimed he didn't tell police about this when they questioned him because he'd thought it was a dream, and it wasn't until recently that he'd realized it had really happened.

There were a few problems with Eugene's confession. He couldn't locate where her body had been or how her body was positioned. He also didn't know that the ground had been muddy. So when police asked Eugene if he was dirty when he got up off the ground, and he said he only had a few leaves on his jacket, it didn't fit. It was also obvious that Rita's body had been carried to the site, since there was no mud on her shoes, and Eugene was too weak to have carried her to the spot where she was found. He weighed only ninety pounds and had health issues. The other problem was that he didn't know when Rita had been killed. Eugene told police that he was home by 10:00 p.m. on Friday, but Rita hadn't been killed until 6:00 a.m. on Saturday.

There were too many inconsistencies, and police agreed that the story was made up. Eugene had not killed Rita. He was then sent to the hospital's psychiatric wing for evaluation. The doctors diagnosed him as suffering from a mental deficiency and concluded that he was a defective deviant with a psychopathic personality. He was sent to juvenile court to face the charges that had brought him to police attention.

Theories

This case is completely cold. There are no leads, and the only theories are that a jealous girlfriend might have killed Rita, or an ex-boyfriend might have killed her—although there has never been any evidence to back either up. We don't know what happened to Rita on that Friday night into Saturday morning, and unless someone finds a confession written somewhere or there is a deathbed confession, we will likely never know.

VERMONT

PAULA WELDEN

One of the People to Go Missing
in the Bennington Triangle

....

NUMBER ONE, THIS IS REALLY ABOUT
LETTING THE FAMILIES OF THE VICTIMS KNOW THAT WE
HAVEN'T FORGOTTEN ABOUT THESE CASES AND THAT
THEY'RE STILL A PRIORITY FOR US.

—VERMONT STATE POLICE MAJOR GLENN HALL

Decemeber 1, 1946, had been a rough day for eighteen-year-old Paula Welden, at least according to her roommate, Elizabeth Johnson. Paula, the daughter of wealthy industrialist William Welden and Jean Douglas Welden, was a sophomore at Bennington College in North Bennington, Vermont. She was, by all accounts, a typical student who was just trying to figure out what she wanted to do with her life. But on this winter's day, everything changed.

It was a Sunday afternoon, and Paula decided to go for a hike along the Long Trail, a hiking trail that runs from Vermont's border with Massachusetts

Paula Welden by the Charley Project. *Courtesy of Wikimedia Commons by permission*

all the way to its border with Canada. Paula had just finished her shift at the school's dining hall and stopped by her room to change into walking clothes. She did not take a bag or any money with her. Paula hitched a ride from a local contractor, Louis Knapp, who dropped her off about two miles from the access point for the Long Trail in Woodford Hollow. She was seen walking north along the trail late in the afternoon. She has not been seen since.

98

Bennington College

Small waterway near the entry point of the Long Trail

Near the start of the Long Trail in Bennington, Vermont

Paula was not reported missing by Elizabeth until the next morning, because the girl claimed to think that Paula had gone to the library to study for exams. As soon as the college administrators were notified, they began a search of the campus. The county sheriff was called in to help search for the missing woman. It wasn't until several days later that authorities were made aware of her trip to the Long Trail. Someone who had seen her on the trail recognized her picture in the newspaper and reported the sighting to authorities. The search of her last-known whereabouts began. There were hundreds of volunteers searching for the missing woman. Most assumed she had gotten lost in the woods near Glastenbury Mountain.

Paula's father, William, became involved in the search for his daughter and was openly critical of how the case was being handled. William believed that the poor training of the local sheriffs and lack of a statewide police organization contributed to law enforcement's inability to find his daughter. He also started organizing his own searches, and his displeasure with basically everyone involved in the search for his daughter was frequently the focus of the media coverage.

The longer Paula was missing, the more people began to whisper about alternative theories about what might have happened. Perhaps she had decided to run off with a young man to start a new life; maybe she was depressed and went into the woods to kill herself; she may have been kidnapped or murdered. Paula's disappearance has even been linked to the paranormal.

Joseph Citro, author of *Green Mountain Ghosts, Ghouls & Unsolved Mysteries*, coined the term "The Bennington Triangle," an area around Glastenbury Mountain that allegedly has a lot of paranormal activity. Part of the mystique of the area is the five people, including Paula, who went missing in that general location, and that the area has been linked to possible sinister paranormal forces.

Tyler Resch, a local historian and author of *Glastenbury: The History of a Vermont Ghost Town*, believes a more down-to-earth explanation exists. Although he is careful not to promote any scenario as definitive, he does mention that Paula's relationship with her father was stressed, and she could have planned a rendezvous with a boyfriend who was waiting with a car. It would explain the lack of evidence and maybe explain why she was leaving at dusk, or near dusk, to go hiking.

Since there was no statewide law enforcement organization at the time, Vermont's governor, Mortimer R. Proctor, asked for help from the Connecticut State Police, after much pressure from William. Since Paula and her family were from Connecticut, it made sense to ask them for assistance. Detective Robert Rundle and policewoman Dorothy Scoville of the Connecticut State Police scoured the area. Every person who lived along the route that Paula took to the Long Trail was interviewed. They turned up a suspect who had been in the area at the time of Paula's disappearance and who was also in a very worked-up state. He had been fighting with his girlfriend the day that Paula disappeared. Additionally, he was caught lying to investigators on several occasions. On top of that, he allegedly told several people that he could identify Paula's grave within one hundred feet, but investigators could never find any hard evidence to connect this man to Paula. Actually, they couldn't even find any evidence that a crime had been committed.

There was one positive outcome in the disappearance of Paula Welden. Her case highlighted the need for statewide law enforcement, and the Vermont State Police evolved directly from the difficulties in this case.

||||||||||||||||||||||||||||||||||||||||||||||||||||||||||||||||||||||||||||||||||||||

In March 2016, the state police announced an interactive website they are now using to try to gather information on missing cases and unsolved murders in Vermont. http://vsp.vermont.gov/unsolved/ shows the cases on a map and provides links so that people can look at the information and even send anonymous tips to the police at http://vsp.vermont.gov/tipsubmit or email Lieutenant Reg Trayah at reg.trayah@vermont.gov.

||||||||||||||||||||||||||||||||||||||||||||||||||||||||||||||||||||||||||||||||||||||

Opinion
We are now seventy years after the disappearance, and no one has ever found out what happened to Paula that afternoon. There are several possibilities, but they all have weak points. The biggest issue for me that rarely seems to be touched upon is the time. Paula decided to go hiking at around 2:30–3:00 in the afternoon

. . . in December? Tyler Resch uses the term "implausible" when mentioning Paula's plan to go hiking. In December, sunset in the Bennington area would have been around 4:40. She was reportedly unfamiliar with the trail and was not equipped to be out after dark in the winter. All this makes me think she had a plan that didn't involve hiking. Hopefully, she met up with someone, and they took off together to start a new life and hasn't come forward because of all the media attention the case received. Having to face the people who searched and worried about her would be a daunting proposition. Although if she is alive she would be around eighty-eight at the time of this writing, perhaps we may hear something if there is a deathbed confession, either from her killer or from Paula herself. Perhaps Joseph Citro is right, and she ran into the local Bigfoot or aliens or whatever curse is on that land.

THE DISAPPEARANCE OF LYNNE SCHULZE

(Middlebury)

In 1971, Lynne Schulze was an eighteen-year-old freshman at Middlebury College in Middlebury, Vermont. Lynne was an athletic girl who enjoyed the outdoors, but making the difficult adjustment from high school to college was weighing heavily on the petite brunette. She had written home to her family in Simsbury, Connecticut, about being homesick, and according to friends she had been depressed and had talked about faking her own death. No one had taken that seriously though. It was December, and finals were almost over. Lynne had one test left and it was in English drama, a class that she had done well in and enjoyed. For all of her talk of leaving, Lynne had enrolled in spring classes at Middlebury College, so it does appear as though she planned to return.

So on the morning of December 10, 1971, nobody expected Lynne to disappear off the face of the Earth. Lynne's final exam was at 1:00 p.m. that day. At 12:30 p.m., she was seen by a classmate eating a bag of prunes outside All Good Things, a local health food store. She talked about catching the bus to New York, but the bus had already left. Fifteen minutes later, Lynne ran into a friend who was going to the same exam at 1:00 p.m. This friend said that Lynne seemed distracted and was not willing to discuss their upcoming exam. Instead, she was focused on finding her favorite pen. When this friend left for the exam, Lynne was no longer around. Lynne did not make it to the exam.

Another college student claims to have seen Lynne at 2:15 p.m. on Court Street, just across from the bus station and All Good Things. This is the last confirmed sighting of Lynne. Did she leave willingly or did something happen to her? In her dorm, she left behind her wallet with her ID, her clothes, and her sleeping bag. She had approximately $30 on her, and nothing else except the clothes she was wearing (a navy-blue sweater, brown ski parka, jeans, and hiking boots). There was a rumor that she had been seen hitchhiking on Route 7 southbound, but this could not be confirmed.

Lynne was reported missing to the campus police two days later, but her parents were not informed for almost a week. On December 16, 1971, her parents reported her missing to the Middlebury Police Department. However, the disappearance

The Middlebury College Campus in Middlebury, Vermont

The area where Lynne was last seen. The red building on the right was the health store owned by Robert Durst.

was not made public until the *Burlington Free Press* published an article about Lynne's disappearance on January 24, 1972.

Lynne has now been missing for over thirty-seven years without contacting any of her friends or family, not even when her parents died in the 1990s. Her family believes that Lynne died not long after she went missing, and there is little hope that she could be alive. This case was reopened in 1992 and remains active.

Theories

There are people who believe Lynne followed through on that teenage fantasy of running away and starting over as someone new. However, that is a difficult act to successfully pull off and maintain for nearly forty years.

Another theory revolves around the owner of the health food store that Lynne frequented and was across the street from when she was last seen. The owners of All Good Things were Fred Durst and his future wife, Kathleen McCormack. This is of note because Fred Durst has been involved in multiple cases of murder and missing persons.

Kathleen McCormack Durst was last seen on January 31, 1982. She stopped by a friend's house unexpectedly after a dinner party in Connecticut. She left her friend's house to go see Durst, then she planned to have drinks with another friend in New York. Durst said they spoke, and he dropped her off at the train station. No one has seen her since.

Susan Berman was a friend of Durst's who helped him with an alibi during the investigation of Kathleen's disappearance. On December 24, 2000, Susan was shot execution style in her Los Angeles home. At this time it was known that Durst was in California, although he did fly back to New York before her body was found. Officials believe that she was killed because the investigation into Kathleen McCormack Durst's disappearance had been reopened.

In order to avoid the police, who wanted to talk with him about the murder of Susan Berman, Durst moved to Galveston, Texas, and pretended to be a woman. During his time in Galveston, Durst's neighbor, Morris Black, was murdered and chopped up, and the pieces were thrown into Galveston Bay. Durst was arrested on October 9, 2001, but was released on bail. He then skipped town, missing a court hearing, and was caught shoplifting in Pennsylvania on November 30. He was tried for Black's murder but was acquitted after claiming it was self-defense.

There was also evidence found that during the time he was a fugitive, he stalked a friend of his first wife who had publicly accused Durst of murdering Kathleen and his brother, with whom he had a contentious relationship. He has also been linked to the disappearance of Karen Mitchell of Eureka, California, in November 1997. The FBI even looked into Durst for the Gilgo Beach Killer murders on Long Island, but they couldn't link him to the murders. That case is still unsolved.

In 2015, Durst cooperated with filmmakers for a six-part HBO documentary, *The Jinx: The Life and Deaths of Fred Durst*. During the filming, he apparently unwittingly confessed to murder when he went to the bathroom while still wearing his microphone. Durst was shaken when the filmmaker, Andrew Jarecki, showed him the incriminating evidence, including the letter sent to police alerting them to Susan Berman's murder, with "Beverly Hills" misspelled the same way he had spelled it (and in the same style of lettering) in a letter Durst sent to Berman's son. Durst excuses himself to the bathroom, where he is recorded as saying, "There it is. You're caught! What the hell did I do? Killed them all, of course." Durst has been arrested for the murder of Susan Berman and is facing the death penalty in California.

This is the man who was just across the street from Lynne Schulze when she was last seen. Perhaps that is a coincidence, as Durst's lawyer claims; if so, Durst is truly jinxed as the HBO documentary claims.

If you have any information about Lynne Schulze, please contact the Middlebury Police Department (Lieutenant Reg Trayah at reg.trayah@ vermont.gov) or go to http://vsp.vermont.gov/tipsubmit if you wish to remain anonymous.

PARANORMAL AND
UNEXPLAINED
PHENOMENA

RAMTAIL FACTORY SITE—GHOSTS

TUCKED AWAY IN WESTERN RHODE ISLAND IS A SMALL,
ONE-OF-A-KIND LOCATION IN THE UNITED STATES. THE
FORMER FOSTER WOOLEN FACTORY, OR THE RAMTAIL
FACTORY SITE AS IT IS NOW FREQUENTLY CALLED, IS THE
ONLY OFFICIALLY HAUNTED SPOT IN THE UNITED STATES.

The Story

The story began in 1799, when William Potter purchased some land along the Ponagansett River. He built his woolen factory and prospered. In 1813, he expanded the operations at the mill and offered partnerships to his two oldest sons and his son-in-law, Peleg Walker. Peleg was responsible for the mill overnight, while

The grave of Peleg Walke

The path to the Ramtail Factory site

One of the remaining walls of Ramtail

A small cellar at the site

William and his sons managed the mill and its daytime operation. At first, the partnership was happy, and things were going well for everyone. However, Peleg grew discontented with his position. He was spending his nights patrolling the site and was responsible for ringing the bell that called everyone to work in the morning. He had little time with his wife and plenty of time to dwell on what he felt was an unfair situation. Peleg became irritable and argumentative. He finally decided to confront William Potter and his other business partners, but the meeting did not go well, and there was a heated argument. People reported hearing Peleg say, "One of these days, you'll have to take the keys from a dead man's pocket!" He then stormed off. Perhaps this was Peleg indicating he was suicidal or that working the night shift was killing him. No one had the chance to find out.

On the morning of May 19, 1822, the usual bell did not chime. When the mill workers went to investigate, they found the mill locked up and no sign of Peleg. Entering the mill through an open window, they found the thirty-five-year-old's body dangling from the bell's rope, and in his pocket was the key to the mill. Just as he had said it would be. While some accepted this as a suicide, there were rumors of foul play.

Peleg was quickly buried in the family plot, but from the time of his death, there were sightings of Peleg walking the grounds. He was usually seen all in white and carrying his lantern, still watching over the mill. The mill would also spontaneously start up in the middle of the night, and it was reported that the

111

Some of the remains of the former factory town

mill's waterwheel was observed running backward against the flow of the current. The bell began to toll in the middle of the night. It became such a problem that the rope was removed so no one could ring it; however, this did not stop the clanging. They finally removed the bell from the site. However, they apparently couldn't remove Peleg, and the sightings continued. People were terrified and exhausted, and they left.

By 1840, the mill was closed. People were unwilling or unable to live in the area due to their fears, and the rumors had spread so that new people did not come to work at the mill. In 1873, the mill was destroyed by fire, leaving only crumbling walls. In 1885, it was listed in the Rhode Island state census as haunted.

Paranormal investigators (and the curious) continue to visit Ramtail in search of Peleg Walker's ghost. There have been reports of people still hearing the bell tolling, and white balls or streaks of light seen in the woods around the ruins of the mill. Some people have even claimed to hear footsteps when there is no one near. Whether you believe or not, Ramtail has been recognized by the government as haunted.

||||||||||||||||||||||||||||||||||||||||||||||||||||||||||||||||||||||||||

Author's note:

I visited the Ramtail site on a bright, sunny afternoon, not a great time for ghosts. However, I did have an odd experience in the woods that day. While walking toward the ruins, I had an owl swoop down just in front of me, twice. Not a ghost, but still odd for a bright, sunny day. The woods in the area were also creepily quiet. When walking through the woods there is usually a lot of noise: birds, squirrels, and other critters. I was able to wander (mostly lost) for over an hour, and the only thing I heard in that time was my owl friend. After I had visited the mill site and started walking back, I started hearing the birds and was stalked by a noisy little chipmunk. So I can't confirm any ghost tales here.

||||||||||||||||||||||||||||||||||||||||||||||||||||||||||||||||||||||||||

THE BETTY AND BARNEY HILL ABDUCTION—ALIENS

···

DEEP THROAT: MISTER MULDER, WHY ARE THOSE LIKE
YOURSELF, WHO BELIEVE IN THE EXISTENCE OF
EXTRATERRESTRIAL LIFE ON THIS EARTH, NOT DISSUADED BY
ALL THE EVIDENCE TO THE CONTRARY?
MULDER: BECAUSE ALL THE EVIDENCE TO THE CONTRARY IS
NOT ENTIRELY DISSUASIVE.
DEEP THROAT: PRECISELY.

—THE X-FILES (SEASON 1, EPISODE 1)

On a cold, rainy November evening, a most unusual meeting was held at the Peirce Memorial Unitarian Universalist Church in Dover, New Hampshire. It was November 7, 1965, and on this night Betty and Barney Hill came forward to share their side of a story that had been published in the *Boston Traveller*, a newspaper that was absorbed into the *Boston Herald* in 1967. This was their chance to tell their side of what happened to them four years earlier. According to John Fuller, author of *The Incident at Exeter* and *The Interrupted Journey*, the church was packed that Sunday evening. The 400-seat church was overflowing with curious people despite the inclement weather.

This story started in early September 1961. Barney, a thirty-nine-year-old African American postal worker, decided to surprise Betty, a forty-one-year-old white social worker, with a surprise, spur-of-the-moment vacation. They packed up their 1957 Chevrolet Bel Air, grabbed their dog, Delsey, and headed off to Niagara Falls. They planned a leisurely trip. After visiting the falls, they went up to Montreal before heading back toward their home in Portsmouth, New Hampshire. The Hills had decided to head home on September 19. They were running low on funds, and the weathermen were forecasting a storm. So they left on that Tuesday evening to drive through the night. Just after they crossed the border into the US, they stopped at a restaurant in Colebrook, New Hampshire, at around 10:00 p.m.

A night shot of Route 3 in Lincoln, New Hampshire

They got back on the road and headed south on Route 3. After about thirty minutes of driving, they noticed a strange light in the sky. Barney at first thought it was a satellite that was off course, and he pulled over to take a look at it with his binoculars. Betty was convinced that it wasn't a satellite, and after looking in the binoculars, Barney agreed. They continued heading south, but Betty kept an eye on the light, which had turned and was now going the same direction they were. Barney kept trying to come up with rational explanations, but the longer they drove, he knew this wasn't something he'd ever encountered before.

When they got to Lincoln, New Hampshire, just past the Indian Head Resort, he stopped the car in the middle of the road. Indian Head is a formation at the top of Mount Pemigewasset, and they were near Natureland, a popular tourist stop, but at this time of night the road was deserted. Barney got out of the car with the binoculars and looked at the object. While he was trying to get a look at it, the craft swung back around until it was about one hundred feet away from them. The craft was as wide across as the distance between telephone poles, and it was saucer shaped. Barney could see a double row of windows that curved around the object. He walked toward the ship and noticed that it was making no sound—there was no noise coming from the craft. Trying to get even closer, he walked out into a field. When he was about fifty feet away, he lifted the binoculars, and through the windows he could see dozens of figures staring down at him. Barney saw all but one of the figures look down at something below the windows, and the craft started lowering, getting closer.

The dress Betty was wearing on the night of the encounter (note the swatches removed for testing)

By this time, Betty, who had remained with the car, was screaming for Barney to come back. Suddenly, Barney snapped out of the near trance he was in and ran back to the car. Both of them were pretty nearly hysterical. They drove off, panicked. They could no longer see the saucer, but they also couldn't see the stars. Shortly, a strange beeping was coming from the rear of the car, and the stars were again visible. Both described a "tingling drowsiness" come over them, then everything went hazy.

They heard the beeping as they again became aware. When they saw the road signs they were thirty-five miles south of where they had been. They kept heading south, and by the time they'd reached Concord, about sixty-five miles from Lincoln, they were again feeling clear headed.

They arrived home, but it was far later than they had expected. The sun was coming up, and when they tried to check their watches, both timepieces were dead. They had very little memory of what had happened to them, and they were missing approximately two hours of time. Both were feeling uneasy, but unable to remember why. They slept until that afternoon.

The Hills each handled the situation very differently: Betty was curious and excited, while Barney wanted to pretend the whole thing never happened. Betty is the one who contacted the United States Air Force about their sighting, though she was not completely forthcoming about their experience, fearing that their story was too fantastical and would be denounced as a hoax. The air force dismissed the sighting. They believed that Betty and Barney had mistaken Jupiter, which had been very bright that night, as an unidentified flying object, or UFO. The information was still passed on to Project Blue Book, an infamous UFO study by the air force from 1952 to 1970.

Betty also began researching UFOs, and she made contact with members of NiCAP, the National Investigations Committee on Aerial Phenomena. She told them a more detailed and accurate account than she had provided to the air force, and they found her story credible. Meanwhile, Barney was doing his best to forget about the incident and continue on normally. Unfortunately, things were far from normal for the couple. Betty began having troubling dreams about what happened that night—dreams so vivid they haunted her waking hours. At the same time,

A dirt road in the region of the Hills' abduction

Barney's preexisting health problems—stomach ulcers and hypertension—became increasingly worse. He was also having increasing problems with anxiety.

In November 1962, the Hills attended a lecture at their church by Captain Ben H. Swett of the US Air Force. After the program, the Hills spoke to Swett about hypnosis, one of the topics he'd discussed that day. They told him their story and asked if he could hypnotize them to help regain the memory of their lost time. Captain Swett refused because he was only an amateur, and he advised that they should seek out a professional. Barney consulted with the psychiatrist he had started seeing and was referred to Benjamin Simon, a Boston psychiatrist. Both Betty and Barney saw Dr. Simon for several months as they tried to recapture the memories of that night. Their stories were shocking at that time but are now a more familiar tale to those familiar with UFO lore.

Barney's Story

Under hypnosis, Barney recalled that after he had heard the beeping from the back of the car, he felt compelled to turn off the highway onto a dirt side road. Waiting for them were six men blocking the road. The car stalled and three of the men came to them and told them not to be afraid. Then the couple was compelled to enter the spaceship. Here they were separated. Barney was brought to an exam room, where invasive procedures were performed on him. He reported being anally probed as well as having skin scrapings and a sperm sample taken. Barney reported he heard Betty and the being they thought of as "the Leader" talking.

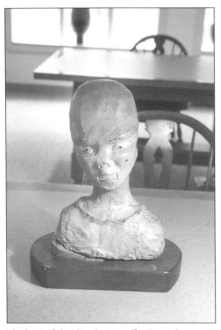

The bust of the alien being, affectionately referred to as Junior, sculpted by Marjorie Fish

Both Betty and Barney remember the communication to be telepathic, since they never saw their abductors' mouths move. The couple was then escorted back to the car. They watched the craft take off before they drove back to the main road to continue on their way home.

Betty's Story

Betty's account matches up pretty closely with Barney's and only varies slightly from the vivid dreams she had after their encounter.

She recounted being forced up the ramp that led to the ship's interior, and remembered arguing with "the Leader" about being separated from Barney. "The Leader" explained that it would take too long to do both exams if they stayed together. Another being, "the Examiner," told Betty they were trying to find the differences between humans and themselves. He took samples of her hair, fingernails, and skin scrapings. He then jammed a needle into her stomach to test her nervous system. According to Betty, the pain was intense, but "the Leader" waved a hand in front of her face and her pain vanished.

She spoke with "the Leader," and he showed her a book with star charts and strange writing. He told her she could keep the book, only to have it taken from her as she left the ship. "The Leader" also showed her a 3-D star chart where he was from, and after hypnosis she was able to draw the map that she saw. She was then reunited with Barney as they left the ship. They watched the ship take off, then continued the drive home.

It was shortly after these sessions that the reporter from the *Boston Traveller* received an audio tape of a UFO meeting the Hills had attended in November 1963. He also got his hands on interviews the Hills had done with UFO investigators, and he found that Betty and Barney had gone through hypnotherapy with Dr. Simon. The story was front-page news for the *Traveller* and was picked up by UPI (United Press International), spreading the story around the world.

After the hypnosis sessions, Dr. Simon believed that the recollections were mere delusions inspired by Betty's dreams. In a reversal of his previous position, Barney disagreed and was now fully convinced that he and Betty had been taken and experimented on by these alien life forms. The hypnotherapy was a success, though, since it relieved the postabduction anxiety they were suffering.

The graves of Betty and Barney Hill in Kingston, New Hampshire

The Betty Hill marker (with tribute) in Greenwood Cemetery

Barney Hill's marker

The marker for the family's plot

After the story was released to the public, Betty and Barney cooperated with author John Fuller on his book *The Interrupted Journey*, which was published in 1966. The Hills maintained for the rest of their lives that the abduction took place. Sadly, Barney died in 1969 of a cerebral hemorrhage; he was only forty-six. Betty lived on for thirty-five years after Barney's death. She died in 2004 of lung cancer at the age of eighty-five.

Theories

While many people believe that the Hills were abducted by aliens, the story has drawn a large number of skeptics. One critic notes that the Hills had been driving for an extremely long time, and since they drove all night they would have been sleep deprived. The Jupiter theory is again brought up. The planet would have matched the position of the light they saw, and on the twisty nature of Route 3, it can play tricks on the perception. It is also noted that the nature of the encounter became more intense just before they reached Indian Head. This lines up with a bright spotlight that had been recently installed (1959) on the top of Cannon Mountain, and, again fitting with this theory, the spot just south of Indian Head where the Hills lost sight of the lights is the same area where the Cannon Mountain light disappears from view on the road. Did Betty and Barney just see these lights, and did their exhausted minds just add to their confusion and fear?

Betty's sister had seen UFOs before; maybe that was enough to plant that suggestion in their overtired brains. Then Betty's dreams built on that fear to the point that they had a shared false memory.

It has also been brought up that as an interracial couple, the Hills would have been facing additional stress from the negative reactions people would have to their relationship. This additional stress could have triggered hallucinations in their fatigued state. Dr. Simon did not feel that this was a factor, nor did Betty, who said they'd had a happy marriage with the support of family and friends.

There is also the similarity of the description of their abductors. *The Outer Limits* had an episode, "The Bellero Shield," that depicted extraterrestrials as the aliens that abducted the Hills. This was aired on TV just two weeks before they were hypnotized. When asked about this, Betty said they had never watched the show. There are also similarities with other fifties-era science fiction TV shows and movies. This could be coincidence; there are only so many ways a humanoid creature can be described, and there is bound to be similarities in any description, or did the images filter into their subconscious minds?

Certainly, it is nearly impossible to conclusively prove or disprove the encounter, unless a third party came forward as an eyewitness. Even then, it isn't likely to be proof enough for either side to debunk or prove it.

I do know that even today, with better lighting and higher traffic, Route 3 is still a dark, lonely road at night. Perfect to induce paranoia, or the perfect place to abduct someone without witnesses.

Historical marker in Lincoln, New Hampshire

Undoubtedly the Hills have had a huge impact on our culture, and they are forever a part of New Hampshire's history. There is even a historical marker in remembrance of the Hills and their trip on the night of September 19, 1961. It is on Route 3 at the Indian Head Resort in Lincoln.

LITTLE ROSE FERRON— RELIGION

....

SOUL OF CHRIST, SANCTIFY ME. BODY OF CHRIST, SAVE ME.
BLOOD OF CHRIST, INEBRIATE ME.
WATER FROM THE SIDE OF CHRIST, WASH ME. PASSION OF
CHRIST, STRENGTHEN ME.
OH GOOD JESUS, HEAR ME.
WITHIN THY WOUNDS HIDE ME.
PERMIT ME NOT TO BE SEPARATED FROM THEE.
FROM THE MALIGNANT ENEMY DEFEND ME.
IN THE HOUR OF MY DEATH CALL ME.
AND BID ME COME TO THEE.
THAT WITH THY SAINTS, I MAY PRAISE THEE.
FOREVER AND EVER.
AMEN.

—ANIMA CHRISTI PRAYER

Stigmata is a religious phenomenon that affects a chosen martyr. The stigmatic is usually a member of the Christian faith, most often Roman Catholic, who bears the wounds of Christ at his crucifixion. This usually manifests as wounds of the hands or wrists and feet. It can also include a wound on the left side of the torso, where Jesus was pierced by a Roman soldier's lance; some have borne the scars of the crown of thorns that was placed on Jesus's head. There are even reports of a wound on the left shoulder, representing where Jesus had carried the cross, and damage representing the whip marks and other blows suffered before the crucifixion. Most stigmatics have religious visions and are plagued with illness, beyond the wounds they suffer.

Saint Francis of Assisi, the patron saint of Italy, animals, and nature, was the first recorded stigmatic. He developed the stigmata in 1224 while he was having a vision during a fast to prepare for Michaelmas, a day for celebrating the Archangel

A memorial at the entryway of Precious Blood Cemetery in Woonsocket, Rhode Island

Michael's defeat of Satan during the war in heaven. St. Francis suffered the wounds until his death in October 1226.

In the Precious Blood Cemetery in Woonsocket, Rhode Island, lies the grave of Marie Rose "Little Rose" Ferron. Marie Rose was born on May 24, 1902, in Saint-Germain-de-Granthum, Quebec, the tenth child of devout Catholic parents. It is even said that Marie Rose was born in a stable just like Jesus, because her mother had been working in the fields when she went into labor.

Accounts tell that Marie Rose began having visions at a young age (sources range from three to six years old), either just before or slightly after her family moved to Fall River, Massachusetts, in 1906. At thirteen years old, Marie Rose became seriously ill, and as a consequence her right arm and left foot became paralyzed. Her hand recovered after two years when she took holy water during mass. They say her hand regained full range of motion; however, the foot never healed, and she needed crutches to walk.

Marie Rose was depressed about her physical limitations (she also suffered from tetanus and intestinal issues), especially because she was unable to attend school. She devoted herself to her religious beliefs and chose to accept her suffering as a vocation. She dedicated her pain as an offering to lessen the pain of others.

In 1925, the family moved from Fall River to Woonsocket, Rhode Island, and within a year Marie Rose began to show the signs of the stigmata. She suffered all the wounds of the crucifixion (hands, feet, side, head, and scourging) and bore the pain of others to lessen their burden. For example, her sisters claim that Marie Rose took on their pain of childbirth. Marie Rose even bilocated, being in two places at once, to be in the room with one of her sisters who was having a particularly difficult labor, yet she was still at home in her bed suffering her sister's labor pains.

Marie Rose was a "victim soul"—she suffered to help others find healing and faith. She had frequent visitors while bedridden in her parent's home and had people sending her letters asking for cures or blessed medals. There were also people who claim that Marie Rose visited them through bilocation. As well as curing people or easing their pain, Marie Rose was credited with bringing people back to the church after years of indifference or disbelief. It was also reported that she appeared at missions all over the world after her death.

As well as the stigmata wounds, her family reported that for the last eleven years of her life, Marie Rose ate no solid food other the Eucharist at Holy Communion. At one point a priest decided to test her and gave her unconsecrated wafers, which made her immediately ill. There was also a three-month period of time about four years before her death that Marie Rose didn't drink any water either, claiming that God alone was sustaining her.

There were also reports that the blood that seeped from her wounds would, at times, smell like roses, and if you came into contact with the blood, the scent of roses would linger on your skin for more than a day.

When Marie Rose was twenty-six years old, she correctly predicted that she would die at the age of thirty-three, just as Jesus had. The date was May 11, 1936,

The grave of Marie Rose Ferron

and she was later buried under a French-inscribed stone in the Precious Blood Cemetery. Despite her death, there are some who claim she has visited and comforted them from heaven, and there have been several attempts to have Marie Rose canonized, but at this time there are no public plans for the church to begin the process of declaring her a saint.

Theories

Marie Rose was frequently examined by doctors, and there was no evidence of her having any physical cause for any of her maladies, and no one has been able to prove that she was faking her symptoms. This leaves two other possibilities. The first is that she had somehow managed to make herself sick through the power of her mind, or, second, this was really a gift—torment from God. Without any scientific answers, it just comes down to a matter of faith.

Marie Rose Ferron by Catholic Web. *Courtesy of Wikimedia Commons by permission*

AMERICA'S STONEHENGE—
ARCHEOLOGY

Just a few miles north of Salem, New Hampshire, lies the remains of a settlement about 4,000 years old. The site, now called America's Stonehenge, has series of stone structures spread out over thirty acres. The site is fascinating; you have old stone structures that have been built from the rocks that litter the terrain. There is a giant astronomically aligned calendar that spans over twenty acres of this New Hampshire forest. The calendar has strategically placed stones that line up with astronomical events such as the equinox sunrise and the winter and summer solstices, among others. There is even a huge "sacrifice table" with a groove carved around the edge to drain the blood away. Set up nearby, the sacrificial stone is in what is called the "Oracle Chamber": a hidden room set up like an echo

A small hut structure at America's Stonehenge

A roofed walkway

The stone "Sacrifice Table"

A path through the rocks

The path to the "Oracle Chamber"

One of the man-made caves

The stone "Sacrifice Table"—note the grooves carved into the stone for drainage

chamber so that during ceremonies, someone could be hidden away from sight and create a disembodied voice that wafted up from under the sacrificial table.

No one knows who lived at this settlement or why the area was deserted, but in 1937 it was given a new purpose. William Goodwin, an insurance company executive and amateur archeologist, purchased the land and began excavating the site. Goodwin believed that Irish Cudlee monks had come across the Atlantic around 4,000 years ago and created the site. He thought that the building structures and stone placements were reminiscent of architecture from pre-Columbian Bronze Age Europe. Unfortunately, in his exuberance over his find, he "fixed" the placement of some of the stones to match with what he believed the site had been. So we can't truly know what was at the site originally, thus throwing into doubt Goodwin's findings.

Curtis Runnels, a professor of archeology in the College of Arts and Sciences (CAS) at Boston University, does not believe that America's Stonehenge was built by the Celts in ancient times. There have been no finds of Bronze Age artifacts that European settlers would have used. As Runnels said, "The whole point of having a specialized science such as archeology is that we've determined certain methods of figuring out how we know what we know. If you have a Bronze Age site in, say, Great Britain, near Stonehenge . . . you're going to find artifacts of bronze, tin, copper, gold, and silver, and they will have distinct forms that are easily recognized. . . . They haven't found anything like this. I'm just an old-fashioned empirical archeologist. I want to see evidence."

Many archeologists believe the stones on the site to be stones left there by local farmers in the eighteenth and nineteenth centuries. Even the sacrificial stone table has been questioned. The grooves carved into the stone resemble lye-leaching stones that many farms in the area used to extract lye from wood ashes to make soap.

So the two sides disagree about what the site was and who lived there, but they do agree that it was once a settlement either of ancient European visitors or a Native American tribe. Whichever side you choose to believe, one thing is certain: the area once known as Mystery Hill is still a mystery for us today.

CONCLUSION

While researching the stories for this book, I came across a "true crime comedy" podcast called *My Favorite Murder*. The hosts of the podcast, Georgia Hardstark and Karen Kilgariff, talk about different crimes they've researched (well, sort of) in a very light-hearted manner. Everything from serial killers to weird stuff that listeners have found in the walls of their homes is covered.

They frequently offer advice so their listeners can "Stay Sexy and Don't Get Murdered." One of their frequent refrains is to "stay out of the forest." Not advice I've ever been able to follow, and I'm sure not willing to spend the rest of my life indoors.

Having studied these cases, and others not in this book, I don't think there is any guaranteed way to be safe. Life is risk. We just need to be aware of our surroundings, and try to keep an eye out for others. If you see something, report it to the authorities. New Englanders and people of other rural areas value "minding our own business"—it makes for good neighbors. However, there are times when we must speak up.

So, I'll end this book with a plea. If you have seen anything, know something, or have found something that may involve these cases (or any other), please contact the authorities. Even if the perpetrator has died, there are people who need to know. The families of the victims have been left in a torturous limbo for too long. If you can help them by providing a clue, please do.

Thank you for picking up this book. I hope you have enjoyed it.

—CATHY MCMANUS

BIBLIOGRAPHY

"1582DFVT—Lynne Kathryn Schulze." Doe Network: International Center for Missing and Unidentified Persons. www.doenetwork.org/cases/1582dfvt. html. Accessed September 27, 2016.

Allen, Mel. "The Day Kurt Newton Disappeared | Yankee Classic." *New England Today*, March 30, 2018. https://newengland.com/today/living/new-england-history/kurt-newton-disappearance/. Accessed March 3, 2017.

Associated Press. "Historic 1962 Heist Still Unsolved." *Cape Cod Times*, January 5, 2011. www.capecodtimes.com/article/20020815/NEWS01/308159982. Accessed September 27, 2016.

Blanco, Juan Ignacio. "Robert Dale Segee." Murderpedia, the Encyclopedia of Murderers. http://murderpedia.org/male.S/s/segee-robert-dale.htm. Accessed September 27, 2016.

Boser, Ulrich. *The Gardner Heist: The True Story of the World's Largest Unsolved Art Theft*. New York: Harper, 2010.

Carpenter, Jason. "A Fiendish Murder: The Rhode Island Cold Case You Never Heard Of." *The Asylum Antiquarian*, May 16, 2016. https://medium.com/the-asylum-antiquarian/a-fiendish-murder-the-rhode-island-cold-case-you-never-heard-of-e353771e8bcc#.w0949wl5a. Accessed September 27, 2016.

Connor, Myles, and Jenny Siler. *The Art of the Heist: Confessions of a Master Thief*. New York: Collins, 2010.

D'Agostino, Thomas, and Arlene Nicholson. *Abandoned Villages and Ghost Towns of New England*. Atglen, PA: Schiffer, 2008.

"Death Row Roster." Florida Department of Corrections. www.dc.state.fl.us/InmateReleases/list.asp?DataAction=Filter. Accessed September 27, 2016.

Dershowitz, Alan M. *Reversal of Fortune: Inside the von Bülow Case*. New York: Random House, 1986.

Donoghue, Mike, and Adam Silverman. "Police: Durst 'Most Interesting' Link to Schulze Case." *Burlington Free Press*, March 25, 2015. www. burlingtonfreepress.com/story/news/local/2015/03/24/middlebury-police-durst-update/70378078/. Accessed September 27, 2016.

"Frank Bradley." Simsbury Volunteer Fire Company. http://simsburyfire.org/memoriam/frank-bradley. Accessed September 27, 2016.

Fuller, John G. *Incident at Exeter: The Interrupted Journey; Two Landmark Investigations of UFO Encounters Together in One Volume.* New York: MJF Books, 1996.

Ginsburg, Philip E. *The Shadow of Death: The Hunt for a Serial Killer.* New York: Scribner, 1993.

"Harold Israel, 1924." *Hartford Courant*, April 28, 2014. www.courant.com/courant-250/moments-in-history/hc-250-trial-surprises-gallery-20140411-001-photo.html. Accessed September 27, 2016.

"Hartford Circus Fire Memorial." The Hartford Circus Fire ~ July 6, 1944: Memorials. www.circusfire1944.com/memorials.html. Accessed July 7, 2018.

"In Search of Mattie Hackett." *Bangor Daily News*, May 24, 2010. http://bangordailynews.com/bdn-maine/community/in-search-of-mattie-hackett. Accessed September 27, 2016.

Kaell, Hillary. "'Marie-Rose, Stigmatisée de Woonsocket': The Construction of a Franco-American Saint Cult, 1930–1955." *Historical Studies* 73 (April 23, 2007): 7–26.

Katz, Hélèna. *Cold Cases: Famous Unsolved Mysteries, Crimes, and Disappearances in America.* Santa Barbara, CA: Greenwood, 2010.

Knox, James, dir. *Dark Minds.* Season 1, episode 1, "The Valley Killer." By James Knox and Colette Sandstedt. Aired January 30, 2012, on Investigation Discovery.

Kurkjian, Stephen A. *Master Thieves: The Boston Gangsters Who Pulled Off the World's Greatest Art Heist.* New York: PublicAffairs, 2016.

"Kurt Ronald Newton." The Charley Project. http://charleyproject.org/case/kurt-ronald-newton. Accessed July 8, 2018.

Lambert, Lane. "Ex-con Myles Connor Wants to Set the Record Straight about His Life of Crime." *Wicked Local*, April 21, 2009. www.wickedlocal.com/ x77787159/Ex-con-Myles-Connor-wants-to-set-the-record-strait-about-his-life-of-crime. Accessed February 15, 2017.

"'Little Rose' Ferron: Stigmatist, Martyr of Love, of Quebec, Canada, and Woonsocket, Rhode Island, 1902–1936." Little Rose Ferron. http:// marieroseferron.com/. Accessed September 27, 2016.

MacEachern, Frank. "Matthew Margolies Cold Case: The Killing That Shook Greenwich." *Greenwich Time*, September 20, 2011. www.greenwichtime. com/news/article/Matthew-Margolies-cold-case-The-killing-that-2176147. php#photo-1589817. Accessed September 27, 2016.

"Making Off with Cape Cod Capital." Postal Inspectors: The Silent Service. Smithsonian National Postal Museum. http://postalmuseum.si.edu/ inspectors/a5p5.html. Accessed September 27, 2016.

"Marie Rose Ferron—American Mystic, Stigmatic and Visionary (1902–1936)." Mystics of the Church, March 2010. www.mysticsofthechurch.com/2010/03/ marie-rose-ferron-american-mystic.html. Accessed September 27, 2016.

McCanna, Ben. "Still Missing: Parents Never Give Up When Children Disappear." *Kennebec Journal and Morning Sentinel*, February 5, 2012. www. centralmaine.com/2012/02/05/still-missing-parents-never-give-up-when-children-disappear_2012-02-04. Accessed March 03, 2017.

Muise, Peter. "The Ghost of Ram Tail Mill." New England Folklore, April 20, 2015. http://newenglandfolklore.blogspot.com/2015/04/the-ghost-of-ram-tail-mill.html. Accessed September 27, 2016.

"The Mystery of the Hartford Circus Fire Still Lingers, 74 Years Later." New England Historical Society, January 03, 2011. www. newenglandhistoricalsociety.com/mystery-hartford-circus-fire-still-lingers-70-years-later/. Accessed September 27, 2016.

"Natanis Point Campground." Natanis Point Campground. www. natanispointcampground.com/. Accessed March 03, 2017.

Ocker, J. W. *The New England Grimpendium*. Woodstock, VT: Countryman, 2010.

"Paula Jean Welden." The Charley Project. http://charleyproject.org/case/ paula-jean-welden. Accessed September 27, 2016.

"Pawtucket Stabbing Has Police Baffled." *Lewiston Daily Sun*, February 4, 1947. https://news.google.com/newspapers?id=_ Z0gAAAAIBAJ&sjid=Q2gFAAAAIBAJ&pg=6627,2585616.

Resch, Tyler. *Glastenbury: The History of a Vermont Ghost Town*. Charleston, SC: History Press, 2008.

Robinson, Rebecca. "After 60 Years, Student's Fate Remains a Legendary Mystery." *Bennington Banner*, January 12, 2006. www.benningtonbanner. com/localnews/ci_4753281. Accessed September 27, 2016.

"Saint Mariam Baouardy (St. Mariam of Jesus Crucified)—the Lily of Palestine." Mystics of the Church, July 2010. www.mysticsofthechurch.com/2010/07/ blessed-mariam-baouardy-little-arab-and.html. Accessed September 27, 2016.

Skidgell, M. "The Cause and Origin of the Hartford Circus Fire: A Study of the Investigations." The Hartford Circus Fire ~ July 6, 1944. July 1, 2015. www. circusfire1944.com/cause-and-origin-study.html. Accessed September 27, 2016.

Souza, Kenneth J. "Seventy-Five Years Later, Little Rose Devotees Still Pray for Sainthood Cause." *The Anchor*, May 13, 2011: 1, 15. https://issuu.com/ the_anchor/docs/05.13.11. Accessed March 3, 2017.

Stoller, Kristin. "Robert Durst Linked to Disappearance of College Student from Simsbury." *Hartford Courant*, March 25, 2015. www.courant.com/ community/simsbury/hc-simsbury-lynne-schulze-robert-durst-20150324-story.html. Accessed September 27, 2016.

Witkowski, Mary. "The Murder of Father Dahme." *Curious Historian*, October 12, 2009. http://blog.ctnews.com/Witkowski/2009/10/12/the-murder-of-father-dahme/. Accessed September 27, 2016.

INDEX

Agnew, Barbara, 76, 77, 80
All Good Things, 103, 105
Allenstown Four, 66, 67
Allenstown, NH, 62, 63, 66, 67
Barrett, William, 47
Bates, Roger, 10
Bear Brook State Park, 62, 63, 66
Begley, Grace, 50
Bennington Triangle, 98, 100
Bennington, VT, 98, 100, 102
Berman, Susan, 105–106
Borden, Abby, 37–42, 45, 46
Borden, Andrew, 37, 39–43, 45, 46
Borden, Emma, 37, 40–42, 44, 45
Boroski, Jane, 78, 79, 81
Boston, Massachusetts, 47, 51, 53, 54, 60, 83, 89, 133
Bowen, Dr., 40, 42, 43
Bowman, Ellen, 24
Branda, Frank, 14

Buck, Colonel Jonathan, 29
Bucksport, ME, 27, 29, 30
Byram River, 8, 9

Chain of Ponds, ME, 31–33
Charley Project, 98
Citro, Joseph, 100, 102
Clarendon Court, 88, 89
Clumber Spaniels, 83
Connecticut State Police, 101
Connor, Myles, 58
Cook, Eleanor, 15
Courtemanche, Bernice, 72, 73
Critchley, Mary Elizabeth, 71, 74
Diaferio, Patricia, 50

Douglas Welden, Jean, 98
Durst, Robert, 104–106

Eisenhower, Dwight, 7
Evans, Robert, 67–68

Fall River, MA, 37, 41, 42, 44–46, 125
Fenway, 52, 53
Fogg Jr., Joseph, 28
Foster, RI, 108
Fried, Ellen, 73

Gardner, Isabella Stewart, 51, 53, 54
Glastenbury Mountain, 100
Goodwin, William, 133
Greenwich, CT, 7–10

Hartford, CT, 12, 13, 16, 18, 60
Hartford, VT, 76
Hobbs Raymond, Elise, 25
Hopkinton, RI, 83– 85

Irish Cudlee Monks, 133
Johnson, Albert, 24, 25
Johnson, Elizabeth, 98

Kelly, Emmett, 12
Kelly, John, 50
Kellyville, NH, 72
Kimberly Newton, 31

Lambert, Frank, 8
Largay, Geraldine, 34
Life Magazine, 47
Lincoln, NH, 115, 116, 122
Little Miss 1565, 16–17
Little Sugar River, 73

Madison Square Garden, 85
Maine State Police, 35
Margolies, Maryann, 8–10
Maxwell, Scott, 66
McCormack Durst, Kathleen, 105
Miazga, Stella, 8

Middlebury College, 103, 104
Miles Lane, 29
Millican, Cathy, 69, 70, 71
Moore, Lynda, 74–76
Morse, Eva, 73, 74
Morse, John, 37, 40, 42, 46
Moxley, Martha, 10–11
Mystery Hill, 134

National Center for Missing and Exploited Children, NCMEC, 63, 68
New Hampshire State Police, 63, 66, 68
Newport, RI, 86–89
Newton, Jill, 31–34
Newton, Ron, 31–35
Nicholau, Michael, 80–81
Northwood Cemetery, 16, 17

O'Nan, Stewart, 17
Oak Grove Cemetery, 43
Oak Hill Cemetery, 30
Oakhill Research, 62, 66, 67
"Ode to Mattie Hackett," 24
O'Neil, George, 84, 85

Paul O'Neil, Paul, 49, 50
Pawtucket, RI, 91, 94
Payne, Jeff, 9–10
Peleg Walker, 108–112
Plymouth, MA, 47–50
Port Chester, NY, 10
Potter, William, 108, 111

Randall, Ronda, 66
Readfield, ME, 24, 25
Red Sox, 53
Resch, Tyler, 101, 102
Richards, Catherine, 71
Richards, Thomas, 50
Rielly, Charles Nelson, 14, 16
Ringling Brothers Barnum and Bailey, 12, 17, 18
Runnels, Curtis, 133

Salem NH, 127
Schena, Patrick, 47

Schrallhammer, Maria, 87–90
Schweitzer, Carol, 66
Segee, Robert, 18
Simsbury, CT, 103
South Hampton, MA, 17
Spooner, Emeric, 28
Sullivan, Bridget, 37, 39–41, 45, 46

The Circus Fire: A True Story of American Tragedy, 17
The Jinx: The Life and Deaths of Robert Durst, 105, 106
The Long Trail, 98–101
Treworgy, William, 27–29

Unde-Freire, Ricaardo G., 48

Vermont State Police, 76, 77, 98, 101
von Auersperg, Ala, 87–90
von Auersperg, Alexander, 87–90
von Auersperg, Prince Alfie, 87
von Bulow, Claus, 87–90
von Bulow, Cosima, 88, 90
von Bulow, Sunny, 86–90

Weldon, William, 98
Westminster Kennel Club, 85
Westover, Gary, 80
Windsor, CT, 16–17
Woodford Hollow, 98
Woonsocket, RI, 124, 125

ABOUT THE AUTHOR

Cathy McManus is a lifelong resident of Maine. She works in the Maine school system as a computer technician and spends much of her free time wandering the cemeteries and old homes in New England. She is a former investigator with one of the ghost-hunting societies in Maine. Cathy is a resident of Farmington, Maine, and enjoys all things geeky.